Amazing Airlines

ISBN 1-4699-9391-0
ISBN-13: 978-1-4699-9391-1

Cover Design by Rajesh Unde
Book Design by Milind Hambarde

"This new book about airlines and airline travel by Aditya Palnitkar is certainly well documented and a must read for anyone not familiar with airlines and air travel, or even for seasoned travelers, who have learned to pretty much take everything in stride, including TSA and security issues.

Even I, who have been flying and litigating all sorts of airline and airplane disaster cases for over 40 years, learned something from this work. That a fifteen year old boy could produce a work of this kind is a real tribute not only to his zeal and interest in his work, but to the depth of the research he had to have done. His use of quotes from other aviation figures throughout the text is a very nice touch."

Gerald C. Sterns, Aviation Attorney, San Francisco

Preface

I fell in love with airlines ever since I flew on my first flight. Aviation excited me like nothing else. I am lucky that my parents love to travel. I have had the opportunity to fly through or visit 24 countries. I used to take detailed notes, photos and videos each time I boarded a flight. For me, the journey was more important than the destination of the flight.

I have read every book I could find on flying. I realized that most books were written for adults, where the organization and the language of the book were difficult to understand for a teenager. I felt that an airline book written in simple language had the potential to fire up imagination in teenagers and young adults. Since a book like this did not exist, I decided to write one.

My purpose in writing this book is to make commercial aviation an interesting topic for teenagers. This book will help unravel the mysteries that surround the airline world.

I do not claim a great vision inspired me to write this book, simply my love for airlines and what airlines represent – "soaring imagination".

I hope you will enjoy Amazing Airlines.

Aditya Palnitkar

Table of Contents

Introduction   1

How does an airline work?   3

*Types of Airlines 5 — Scheduling and Routing 11 — Airline Tickets 17 —
Paperless Boarding 21 — And then the Airline "Fees" 22 — 'Scheduled' Delays 23 —
Red Eye Flights 24 — Airline Food 26*

Airline Crew: The people who make it all happen   29

*Pilots 30 — Language of the Skies 35 — Flight Attendants 36 —
Airline Crew History 39*

Baggage Handling: Where is my bag?   42

*Baggage Handling Basics 44 — Baggage Check-in 45 — Conveyors 46 —
DCVs 46 — Loading the Plane 48 — Making Transfers 49 — Baggage Claim 49 —
Lost Luggage 50*

Airports: The home of airlines   52

*What are airports? 53 — Airport Terminals 53 — Customers and Passengers 55 —
Ground Transportation 56 — Concourses and Terminals 57 — Gates 59 —
Runways 60 — Airport Codes 61 — Airport Lights 61 — Runway Lights 62 —
Fuel 63 — Airport Management 64 — Safety 65 — Airports and the environment 66*

What happens when you fly   68

*Before takeoff 68 — Aircraft maintenance 68 — Flight planning 69 —
Securing the Aircraft 69 — Ground Preparations 69 — Passenger Screening 70 —
Crew Briefing 70 — Cockpit preparations 70 — Safety Checks 71 —
Pre-Boarding 71 — General Boarding 72 — Cell phones and airplanes 72 —
Closing the cabin door 72 — Safety Briefing 73 — Push Back and Taxiing 73 —
De-icing 74 — Takeoff 74 — Air Traffic Control 75 — In flight 75 —
Landing the aircraft 76 — Arriving at the gate 76 — Arrivals 77 —
Final Checklists 77 — Resolving Aircraft Faults 77*

Roger that: Air Traffic Control   78

*Airspace and Air Traffic Control 79 — Phases of flight 81 — Problems 90 —
Call Signs 92 — Air Traffic Control Careers 93*

Inside the cockpit: What are those pilots up to?   94
Before the flight 95 — Boarding 96 — Pushback 97 — Taxi 98 —
Takeoff 99 — Cruise 101 — Descent 103 — Approach 103 — Landing 105 —
Gate Arrival 107 — Shutdown 108 — Resolving Aircraft Faults 108

The airplanes that get us there   109
Bernoulli's Principle 110 — Aerodynamic Forces 111 — Controlling Flight 112 —
Jet Engines 113 — Parts of an airplane 115 — Aircraft Maintenance 122 —
Painting the Aircraft 125 — Airplane liveries 127 — Airplane Makers 128 —
Fly By Wire 129

The scary part of flying   131
Airplanes vs. Cars 132 — Airplane Sounds 135 — Why do airplanes crash? 140 —
The media and airplane disasters 143

The History (and future) of Airlines   144
Wheels up: The world takes flight 144 — The first airlines 146 — The 1920's 146 —
The 1930's 147 — Flying across oceans 148 — After the war 148 —
The jet engine era 150 — Deregulation 151 — Airlines today 152 —
The future of airline travel 153 — Mergers 153 — Baggage Fees 155 —
Automation in Customer Service 155 — Standing Seats 156 — New airplanes 156 —
Resolving Aircraft Faults 157

Author's Note   158

About the Author   159

Acknowledgements   160

More Information   162

Art Credits   164

Index   165

Introduction

If you are planning a trip somewhere close, you could drive your car, ride a train or take a boat, but for longer distances, the odds are you'll be flying. When you fly on an airline, have you ever taken a moment to think how an airline works? Probably not, because very few people actually understand how an airline works.

There are two groups of people. The first group has people who think that getting to their destination by airplane is the most wonderful part of a trip – enjoying every takeoff and every landing. The second group has people who think that flying is only a way of getting from point A to point B. This book is for both the groups – people who already love flying and want to know more, and those who will get to love flying after reading this book.

An airline is a very interesting organization. The complex system of airplanes, employees and schedules just boggles the mind. This book will give you a behind-the-scenes insight into an airline – a fascinating look at the systems that are working to help you fly from place to place. It will also give you a good look at what happens when you fly, what pilots do inside the cockpit, how baggage handling works and more.

Teenagers and young adults will relate to this book the most as it comes from my personal experience and research over a period of 4 years. I have kept the language in the book simple and conversational. There is no set way to read the book. You can read this book from front to back, or back to front, or skip to the chapters that interest you the most. So go ahead, dive in into the world of Amazing Airlines!

All the calculations show it can't work. There's only one thing to do: make it work.

— Pierre Georges Latécoère, early French aviation entrepreneur.

How does an airline work?

Boeing 757 just before landing

So here you are, planning to fly somewhere rather than drive your car, ride a train or take a boat. Airplanes give us the ability to travel long distances in only a fraction of the time it would take by other forms of transportation. If you are traveling by air, you will almost certainly have to fly on one of the many commercial airlines flying to and from your country, unless you have a private jet.

> *"First Europe, and then the globe, will be linked by flight, and nations so knit together that they will grow to be next-door neighbors. . . . What railways have done for nations, airways will do for the world."*
>
> **— Claude Grahame-White, 1914.**

The private jet system is quite easy to understand – load up your bags, get in the aircraft, and off you go! But when it comes to commercial airlines, it's pretty complicated – so much so that it takes an entire book to explain it!

Normally, people travel by air either for business or for pleasure. But whatever the reason, nobody can ignore the fact that people love to travel, as is witnessed by the hordes of travelers at the airport nowadays. Airlines are a very important service in today's world.

An airline's main job is to transport passengers and their luggage to their destination. An airline is like any other service which makes customers lives easier. The smooth functioning of an airline depends on various elements. So get ready to explore the world of airlines - types of airlines, hubs and spokes, codeshares, tickets, schedules, airplane food and more in this chapter.

Type of Airlines

All airlines are different. They are like most businesses, and there is a sort of division between them. Airlines are either publicly or privately owned - however, in many countries, the government owns the airline, known as a state-run airline. An airline's rank is determined by the amount of money it generates, known as revenue. Airlines are classified and categorized as: major, national, regional, low-cost, cargo and charter. If you've flown before, it may be easy for you to tell the difference between the categories (of course, it is unlikely that you would fly cargo). Each of the types of airlines has identifiable features. Normally, the larger airlines offer more destinations and more routes, while the smaller ones offer comparatively less destinations and routes.

Major airlines

These are the big guys of the airline industry. A major airline is defined as an airline that generates more than $1-billion in revenue annually. Some major airlines are American Airlines, Delta Airlines, United Airlines and Air France-KLM.

To save money, American Airlines announced that they will no longer provide pillows during flight.

National airlines

Just a little away from the major airlines, these are airlines with annual operating revenues between $100-million and $1-billion. Some national airlines like KLM are also major airlines. These airlines might serve certain regions of the country, but may also provide long-distance routes and some international destinations. They operate medium- and large-sized jets. These are smaller airlines, so that is why they normally have a smaller number of employees and crew.

National airlines are also called flag carriers. A flag carrier is an airline that represents a country. The airline could be owned by a country or privatized, or a mixture of both.

Alitalia recently entered into a controversy when it stopped a passenger from entering business class because he did not look like a businessman!

Next, let's look at regional airlines.

Regional airlines

Ever wanted to visit a place which few people have ever heard of? Chances are you'll be flying a regional airline. Most airlines overlook small towns, but regional airlines fill in these gaps. Normally regional airlines have smaller aircraft, with a seat capacity of around 60, so they can takeoff from and land on shorter runways.

Larger airlines normally partner with regional airlines to provide service to and from some airports which do not have many passengers.

Belgian regional airline VLM Fokker 50 at Manchester Airport

Regional Airlines often repaint their aircraft fleet in the major airline's livery which they partner with. For example, Continental Connection regional airline partner CommutAir paints its entire fleet in Continental Connection colors. On the other hand, regional airline Gulfstream International Airlines paints none of its aircraft in Continental Connection colors.

There is another type of airline – a low cost one.

Low Cost airlines

A low cost airline is also known as a no-frills airline. As the name suggests, this is a type of airline that generally has lower fares. To make up for revenue lost in decreased ticket prices, the airline may charge for extras like food, priority boarding, seat allocating, checking in baggage, etc.

So how do these airlines offer low fares?

The longest scheduled non-stop commercial flight at the moment is Newark-Singapore, flown by Singapore Airlines with the Airbus A340-500. The duration of the flight averages around 18 hours!

One of the features of a low cost airline is a single cabin class, and even a single type of airplane. Typically, fares increase as the plane fills up, which rewards early reservations. Direct flights, unreserved seating is prevalent on low cost airlines. Low cost airlines fly to less congested secondary airports, sometimes even outside of the city. They fly early in the morning or late in the night to avoid air traffic delays. Not every low-cost carrier may have these features though.

South African low cost airline Kulula

Low cost airlines have been the butt of aviation jokes for ages! But people flock to them because the fares are low, sometimes really low. That is why they are really popular.

Charter airlines

How about flying 'on-demand'? Charter flights are probably the next best thing to having your own private jet!

Commercial flights are scheduled – they leave at regular intervals and anyone can purchase tickets up to the day of departure, however, a charter flight is a little more exclusive. A charter flight is usually booked in advance as transport for a group of tourists, a company or even a wedding.

Although charter airlines typically carry passengers who have booked individually or as small groups to beach resorts, historic towns, or cities where a cruise ship is awaiting them, sometimes an aircraft is chartered by a single group such as members of a company, a sports team, or the military.

Unlike some years ago, today almost anyone can book a charter flight. This is because airlines have opened up their ticket sales to the general public. Most private charter airlines will provide you a personalized price quote for your trip.

The ticket price of a charter airline can be well below cost for the airline. While scheduled airlines can charge a premium price for tickets purchased a few days before departure, secure in the knowledge that seats will continue to fill to the last minute, charter airlines are faced with the opposite situation. People who purchase charter tickets buy them well in advance. With a slimmer profit margin, as the departure date nears, the charter flight will scramble to fill empty seats, offering drastically discounted fares.

A charter flight gives little or no refund on cancellations, because of these reasons. However, many charter airlines allow you to transfer your ticket to another person for a small fee.

Charter airlines have small profit margins and relatively small company sizes. There have been a number of incidents in recent years when charter airlines went bankrupt and left passengers who bought tickets in the lurch.

Now let's look at the last type of airline – cargo airlines.

Cargo airlines

Cargo airlines, as the name suggests, are airlines that transport cargo and nothing else. There are a number of cargo airlines across the globe. These airlines use aircraft to move goods and cargo from place to place. Cargo airlines are also known as air freight carriers. Some well known cargo airlines are FedEx, DHL, UPS and Cargolux.

Normally, cargo airlines use large military airplanes for transporting cargo. This was pioneered by Ukraine's Antonov Airlines in the 1990s. These large cargo aircraft carry goods ranging from mail to heavyweight machines to aircraft parts to different parts of the world. The largest cargo plane in the world is the Antonov An-225, a heavy transport aircraft designed to ferry the Buran space shuttle and components of the Energia rocket.

> *"I've never known an industry that can get into people's blood the way aviation does."*
> **— Robert Six, founder of Continental Airlines**

A number of major international airlines have cargo subsidiaries. These air cargo carriers are operated as a freight and baggage transport division of these airlines.

These are the different types of airlines. The airline industry is just like any other business, meaning that there are numerous types of airlines because their customers have different needs. If you are going overseas for business, you're likely to use a major airline because it has more destinations overseas. A business package sent via FedEx ends up on a cargo plane. A holiday traveler flying between two destinations in the same country may fly a national airline. A person traveling between two small cities is likely to fly on a regional airline or a low-cost airline, because he doesn't want to stop at a major-airline airport for a layover.

Cargo airline FedEx MD-11F landing at Cologne-Bonn Airport, Germany

The shortest scheduled commercial airline flight in the world is a British Airways commuter flight from Westray to Papa Westray in Scotland. The duration of the flight is two minutes, and is flown by a BN-2 Islander aircraft.

Scheduling and Routing

Ever wondered how airlines determine their routes and schedules? Cost, passenger comfort, capacity and revenues are some factors that must be considered while determining schedules and routes. Here are some commonly used models to optimize schedules and routes.

Hubs and Spokes

Sometimes, when you book a ticket, you find that you have to fly to a major city first, and then continue to your destination. This major city is an airline hub. A hub is basically a central airport that flights are routed through, and spokes are the routes that planes take out of the hub airport.

Hubs allow airlines to offer more flights for passengers. Many hubs of the airlines are also situated at airports in the cities of the respective head offices. Some airlines may use only a single hub, while other airlines use multiple hubs. Hubs are used for both passenger flights as well as cargo flights. Many airlines also utilize focus cities, which function almost the same as hubs. Airlines may also use secondary hubs, a term for large focus cities. Most international airlines use a hub-and-spoke network to route their plane traffic.

This hub and spoke system got its name from the bicycle wheel - the center of the wheel is like the airline's hub, and the spokes represent the airline's flights to and from the destinations it serves.

A good example of a hub-and-spoke system is that of an airline which has its hub at Hartsfield Atlanta International Airport. Let's say you are in San Francisco, CA, and want to go to Louisville, KY. There's probably not a lot of demand for a San Francisco to Louisville nonstop flight, so the airline flies you from San Francisco to Atlanta, and then from Atlanta to Louisville via a connecting flight

> *"I fly because it releases my mind from the tyranny of petty things..."*
> **- Antoine de Saint-Exupéry**

where the airline also connects passengers who want to fly to Louisville from other cities onto this flight. So the airline first flies everyone from these cities to Atlanta and then connects them to a flight from Atlanta to Louisville. In this example, Atlanta is the hub and the flights from San Francisco to Atlanta and Atlanta to Louisville are spokes.

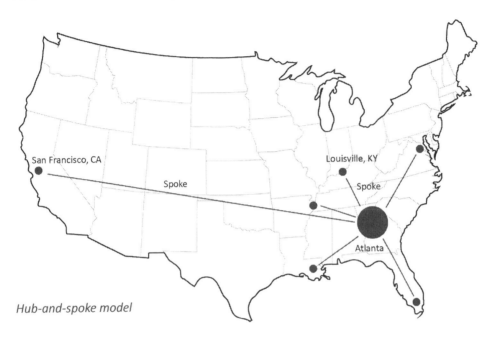

Hub-and-spoke model

Many airlines supplement their hub and spoke model with codeshares (partner flights), normally on a small commuter airline. For example, it would be rather silly to fly passengers who needed to get from Los Angeles to San Francisco through Dallas, the airline's hub. So, these passengers are put on a smaller commuter flight which connects Los Angeles and San Francisco. These commuter flights may also travel between spokes and less desirable locations which do not need to be connected directly to the hub. (We'll see more of this later).

Usually, major airlines have a whole terminal to themselves at their hub airports. Hartsfield Jackson International Airport is the primary hub of AirTran Airways, Delta Air Lines, and Atlantic Southeast Airlines. The Delta Airlines hub is the world's largest airline hub.

Something special in the air.
— American Airlines advertising slogan.

The hub-and-spoke system saves airlines money and gives passengers better routes to destinations. Airplanes are an airline's most valuable asset, and every flight has certain costs. Each seat on the plane represents a portion of the total flight cost. For each seat that is filled by a passenger, an airline lowers its break-even price, which is the seat price at which an airline stops losing money and begins to show a profit on the flight.

There are, of course, disadvantages to a hub and spoke model. Any disruption at the hub, such as bad weather or a security problem, can create delays throughout the system. The overall operating efficiency is also limited by the capacity of the hub. Many airlines choose different cities for hubs, so that two major airlines do not use the same airport as a hub. The airline must also schedule flights very carefully to ensure that all of the spokes are getting the service they need, and to keep passengers content.

Point to Point

The second system airlines use for scheduling flights is the point to point system. Point-to-point transit refers to a transportation system where a plane travels directly to a destination, rather than going through a central hub.

Southwest Airlines in the United States is a primary example of an airline that uses the point-to-point transit model. The advantage of a point-to-point system is that it may minimize connections and travel time, but only if the airline serves the destination via the origination point.

But if a city pair is not served, passengers are out of luck, as there is no way to get to a destination using that airline's route network. Secondly, since there are so many city pairs, it is not possible to find airplanes to serve each city pair often, so frequency of flights is reduced.

Hawaiian Airlines holds the record for the highest number of flight cancellations!

Codeshares

Remember the days when the name on the side of the plane had something to do with the airline you thought you were flying?

While booking a trip from Mumbai, India to Huntsville, AL the other day on delta.com, I discovered that Delta did not fly any of the segments! First, the flights from Mumbai to Paris and Paris to Atlanta were operated by Air France. Notice the word 'operated'? It means that Air France pilots would be flying the plane, and you would get a French meal, even though you booked the flight on Delta's website and got Delta frequent flier miles! Even the next flight from Atlanta to Huntsville was operated by a different airline called Pinnacle Air, which is a small regional airline. But after all this, the flights I flew on still had a long 4 digit Delta flight number!

At the airport, I looked for my flight on the airport monitors. I saw my flight, but a little further, I saw another flight leaving at the same time. Upon further examination I found that the same flight was listed multiple times on the monitor under different airline names!

If I buy a ticket on Delta, shouldn't I expect Delta to fly the airplane? Welcome to the sometimes confusing world of codeshare agreements.

In its simplest form, codesharing works like this: You buy a ticket on Delta for a flight operated by Air France along a route Delta otherwise does not serve.

> *"Nobody who has not been up in the sky on a glorious morning can possibly imagine the way a pilot feels in free heaven."*
> **- William T. Piper, president of Piper Aircraft Corporation**

A codeshare flight is a commercial flight which is operated by one airline, but marketed by others. This concept can be confusing for passengers, but ultimately it can be a valuable service. As a general rule, a flight will be identified as a codeshare flight when tickets are booked, for the convenience of the passenger. This offers you added destinations across the globe.

The concept was pioneered in 1990 by an agreement between American Airlines and Qantas. The two airlines reached a cooperative agreement which merged many of their flights. Essentially, the agreement allowed American Airlines to sell tickets on Qantas flights, and for Qantas to sell tickets on American flights. The result was that each airline could service more areas, without technically expanding its service.

Multiple airlines began to follow suit, and it is not unusual to see three or four airlines all selling tickets on the same flight. The "codesharing" refers to the idea that each airline generates a separate flight code, such as AA625 for "American Airlines Flight 625," so a flight may be identified by multiple codes for passengers, depending on which airline they booked tickets through.

The airline which actually runs the flight is called the "operating carrier." This carrier is responsible for all service provided. Earlier, when people checked in for a flight, they were generally expected to go to the desk of the operating carrier, regardless as to which airline sold the original tickets.

However, in modern times, with space-age integration between airlines, you can go to the counter of the airline that sold you the tickets and check in. Air traffic control identifies the flight by the flight code of the operating carrier, although airport status screens such as arrival and departure boards may list multiple flight codes for the same flight, reflecting the codesharing agreement.

Carriers which sell tickets on other airlines are known as "marketing carriers." Many passengers prefer to stick with one marketing carrier, so that their frequent flier miles and benefits are consolidated. In many cases, a marketing carrier has multiple codeshare agreements, to ensure that customers will get the flight service that they need.

Problems can also arise if you need to change your itinerary or want to change your seat. Most airlines will tell you that you need to contact the carrier that sold you the ticket, rather than the carrier you are actually flying.

While the selling airline is most often responsible for reservations issues, lost or damaged baggage claims are generally submitted to the last airline that handled your luggage at your destination.

But in many cases, competition is diminished by codesharing. Air Canada is the sole airline offering non-stop service between San Francisco and Toronto today and every Air Canada flight is also code shared by their Star Alliance partner, United. But I remember a time not long ago when Air Canada and United both competed on that route. Unfortunately, those days are over and codeshares are here to stay.

American Airlines 777 in Oneworld alliance livery

Airline Tickets

Once you determine your destination, your next step is to call your favorite airline (the one which offers great airline food) and make a reservation on a flight, or book it online (more about e-tickets later). Airlines employ many people who process these reservations and your tickets. There are two types of tickets:

- Paper tickets - This is the conventional ticket that passengers have been using for decades, but not anymore.

- Electronic tickets – This is better known as 'today's ticket'. Many travelers are starting to use electronic tickets, or e-tickets, instead of paper tickets. At the airport, passengers with e-tickets need only obtain their boarding pass by providing the gate agent with a confirmation number and proof of payment (sometimes, they only need to show a photo I.D.).

It is now common for a traveler to pay a fee, assessed by the airline company, for a paper ticket. In fact, many airlines no longer issue paper tickets. IATA (International Air Transport Association) has announced that all IATA-member airlines will no longer issue any paper tickets.

"Flight Reservation Systems decide whether or not you exist. If your information isn't in their database, then you simply don't get to go anywhere."
— Arthur Miller

Take a flight somewhere and look around you. The chances are that the person seated next to you may have paid four times more than you, for the exact same flight. Or maybe you were the sucker and paid four times more than he did! Worse still, many of the people seated in first class probably paid less for their seats than you did for your uncomfortable middle seat way at the very back, next to the toilets, galleys and engines.

Is this fair?

Let's take a look at why the airlines have what seems to be crazy and inconsistent pricing for the same flight. To understand this, you need to think like an airline executive and understand the problems they face.

There are several factors that contribute to the cost of a fare:

- *Competition on Route*
- *Seat Demand*
- *Distance of Route*
- *Seat Supply*
- *Fuel Prices*
- *Purchase date*
- *Class*
- *Flight date and time*

Based on these factors, airlines decide how much to charge you for the flight. So now you know how airline ticketing works.

> *"I technically have two last names, which is a lot of fun when you're making airline reservations."*
> **- Mackenzie Astin**

Overbooking

When you buy a theater ticket, you expect to see a show and not be told, "Sorry, all the seats are taken," when you arrive for the performance. But that's not how airlines operate.

Revenue is what keeps airlines running, and it turns out that the best way for airlines to make money is to ensure that there are as few empty seats on a plane as possible.

When a person doesn't show up for a flight, the seat is left empty and an empty seat is a lost opportunity for revenue.

To deal with this, airlines routinely overbook flights to compensate for no-shows: people who reschedule or opt not to fly. An empty seat on a plane means a loss of revenue to an airline.

Many airlines also employ fancy statisticians to figure out how many seats the airline needs to overbook just to make up for the no-shows.

Normally, if a flight is overbooked and all the people show up, then the airline asks for volunteers to give up their seat, usually for perks like an airline voucher or hotel stays.

E-tickets

When was the last time you used a paper ticket while flying? Most people would reply that they don't remember. This is because they use e-tickets.

An e-ticket carries the same information as a paper ticket. The major difference is an e-ticket is located in an airline's computer database, instead of the passenger's suitcase. It is an electronic record of the traveler's airline reservation, containing information such as the time, date and place of the flight, airport, seat assignment and travel class. At the gate, e-ticket passengers need only show a valid photo identification card such as a passport or driver's license to claim their spot on the aircraft. Once the airline confirms the traveler's information, it issues a boarding pass that the traveler uses to board the plane.

E-ticketing reduces the amount of paper used as well as reduces the costs associated with printing and mailing out tickets.

> *"You cannot get one nickel for commercial flying."*
> *— Inglis M. Uppercu, founder of the first American airline to last more than a couple of months, Aeromarine West Indies Airways, 1923.*

First, a person logs onto a travel website to purchase airline tickets. He might also go through a travel agent who will handle the purchasing of the e-tickets for the customer.

When a ticket is purchased through an online travel site or agency, the airline's computer system receives notification of a ticket purchase along with the passenger's information. Because of this, the airline's computer system must be linked in real time to travel websites and ticket agencies. This real time connection also allows the airline's system to accurately reflect which seats are available on which flights.

Airlines use a computer reservation system to do this. A computer reservations system (CRS) is a computerized system used to store and retrieve information and conduct transactions which is used by airlines. If a company sells tickets for multiple airlines, it is called a global distribution system. These systems were originally designed and operated by airlines themselves, but they were later extended for the use of travel agencies. Some major computer reservations systems are Amadeus, Sabre and Galileo.

After the ticket is purchased, a confirmation e-mail is sent to the customer, confirming the seat numbers purchased and all personal information. No physical ticket is mailed to the customer, however some people print out a copy of the confirmation e-mail.

Upon arrival at the airport, the passenger visits either the airline's service desk or an automated kiosk and gives or punches in his information. The passenger is required to show government issued I.D., such as a passport or valid driver's license in order to receive a boarding pass from the service desk or kiosk.

When a flight is preparing for boarding, the passenger gives his boarding pass to the gate attendant and his government issued I.D. is also double checked to verify the passenger information. After the gate attendant does this, the passenger walks down the jetway into the airplane.

"Air transport is just a glorified bus operation."

— Michael O'Leary, Ryanair CEO

Paperless Boarding

Do you know that when you travel on select airlines, you can have your boarding pass sent right to your mobile phone?

Many airlines give you the option to have your boarding pass sent directly to your mobile device on select flights - saving paper and time.

It's a pretty simple concept. When you check in online for your flight, the airline sends a two dimensional bar code (called QR code) to your phone or PDA. No need to print out a boarding pass from home, no need to stop at the kiosk when you get to the airport.

Conventional airline boarding pass

When you reach security, you flip open your phone and show the bar code to an airport employee, who scans it with a special reader. After you pass security, you go straight to the gate.

And then the Airline "Fees"

While booking your ticket, you should be careful to check for extra airline fees - even if you have found a great deal on an airline. Finding the best deal on a flight has become a lot more difficult, thanks to hefty baggage and service fees that consumers often don't know about until they show up at the airline counter.

Those fees are not part of the ticket price, meaning they can easily go unseen until it's too late for the consumer to change it.

Besides checked bags, some airlines charge fees for seat selection, extra leg room, prime spots in boarding lines, blankets, pillows, drinks and meals!

The first airline to hold a scheduled service was the St. Petersburg-Tampa Airboat Line. The service began in the winter of 1914. One or two passengers sat on wooden seats, and enjoyed fresh Florida air and salt spray in their faces.

'Scheduled' Delays

Ever felt like there's some big conspiracy about flight delays in the airline world? It amazes many people how your plane can be sitting right at the gate, running on time for your flight, and then it somehow becomes an hour and a half delayed.

Don't worry, it's not a conspiracy. Plenty of factors affect whether a flight leaves on time. The most common one is mechanical problems. If your flight encounters any mechanical problem on the ground, the maintenance engineers immediately fix it.

The second one is if your aircraft is needed elsewhere. If your flight has only 50 passengers, and another flight with 200 passengers has some trouble, then your aircraft is used for their flight. Airlines have a rule – always inconvenience the fewest number of passengers.

The third factor is weather. If the weather at your destination city is bad, your flight might get delayed. Sometimes your flight might get delayed even if the weather at the city your aircraft is coming from is bad!

The Federal Aviation Administration (FAA) holds conference calls every two hours to check for any delays and solve them.

> "If the Wright brothers were alive today Wilbur would have to fire Orville to reduce costs."
> — **Herb Kelleher, Southwest Airlines**

Red Eye Flights

While many airports still shut down during the late night hours, airlines continue to grow their number of late-night flight options, also known as red-eye flights. Major airlines offer overnight travel options across the world. Although they're the bane of many weary business travelers, red-eye flights do offer some advantages to airlines and travelers alike.

A red-eye flight denotes any flight moving west to east, against the direction of the sun that occurs overnight, making the traveler experience a period of night that is just a few hours long. The term red-eye is used because of one of the most obvious physical effects of insufficient sleep: irritated, bloodshot eyes. In most cases, red-eye flights depart after 9 p.m. and arrive before 5 a.m. the next day, so flights like transatlantic flights that leave in the afternoon and arrive early the next morning, while still a tiring experience, are not considered red-eye flights.

The disruption to the traveler's sleep cycle is the major disadvantage to a red-eye flight. A five-hour flight that leaves at 10 p.m. and arrives in the early morning makes it impossible for a traveler to get the recommended seven to nine hours of nightly sleep. This is true even if the traveler slept every second from takeoff to landing. Red-eye flights also cause jet lag.

Jetlag is actually caused by disruption of your 'body clock', a small cluster of brain cells that controls the timing of biological functions, including when you eat and sleep. The body clock is designed for a regular rhythm of daylight and darkness, so it's thrown out of sync when it experiences daylight and darkness at the 'wrong' times in a new time zone. The symptoms of jetlag often persist for days as the internal body clock slowly adjusts to the new time zone. Jet lag can take a few days to recover from and can bring symptoms like fatigue, insomnia, headaches, and digestive problems.

GOL Airlines Boeing 737 getting ready for a night departure

eHow.com notes that travelers can take a few steps to lessen the physical impact of a red-eye flight. Seat selection is important. Seats at the back of the plane are the worst, as they do not recline and are usually by the bathroom, ensuring a consistent line of people standing next to their occupants during the flight. Exit row seats also do not recline but usually offer more legroom, and the travelers in front of them are not able to recline either. Window seats are the best for sleep, with the plane wall there for the traveler to lean upon. Carry-on items like a travel pillow, a sleep mask and ear plugs can help a traveler sleep during the quick night. Once at their destination, however, red-eye travelers should avoid sleeping until regular sleeping hours, because even short naps can disrupt one's sleep rhythm. Red-eye flights do offer a few advantages for the traveler. Red-eye flights are cheaper than daytime options in most cases. Hardy business travelers can maximize efficiency, not losing work time before or after the trip, and leisure travelers with limited vacation time can make the most of their allotted days. The airport can be less of a hassle; with fewer people in the check-in and security lines late at night. Fewer flights during late hours means planes are less likely to face congestion delays. Once on the plane, red-eye flights are usually less crowded than daytime flights, so there's plenty of space to find optimal seats, grab pillows and blankets, and get a spot in the overhead luggage bin.

"I'm flying high and couldn't be more confident about the future."
— Freddy Laker, Laker Airways, 3 days before the collapse of Laker Airways, 3 February 1982.

Airplane Food

An airline meal or in-flight meal is a meal served to passengers on board a commercial airliner. These meals are prepared by airline catering services. The first kitchens preparing meals in-flight were established by United Airlines in 1936. These meals vary widely in quality and quantity across different airline companies and classes of travel. They range from a simple beverage in short-haul economy class to a seven-course gourmet meal in long-haul first class.

In-flight catering is an $18 billion worldwide industry employing up to 200,000 people!

The type of food varies depending upon the airline and class of travel. Meals may be served as "one tray" or in multiple courses with no tray and with a tablecloth, metal cutlery, and glassware (generally in first and business classes).

The airline dinner typically includes a main course of vegetables or meat, a salad or vegetable, a small bread roll, and a dessert.

Caterers usually produce alternative meals for passengers with restrictive diets. These must usually be ordered in advance, sometimes when buying the ticket.

LSG Sky Chefs, the world's largest airline caterer, served 427 million meals for 260 airline customers worldwide in 2001.

Meals must generally be frozen and heated on the ground before takeoff, rather than prepared fresh. Higher altitudes alter the taste of the food and the function of the taste buds. The food may taste "dry and flavorless" as a result of the pressurization inside the airplane, and thirsty passengers drink alcohol when they ought to drink water. The palate grows practically numb when it's 35,000 feet in the sky, and that's why everyone says all airline food tastes the same. Some airlines are starting a 'hot food' service to attract passengers.

Cheap seat cuisine has long been the subject of airline jokes and complaints, and for good reason. It pays to be informed as quality and availability of airline food varies widely from airline to airline and flight to flight. As a rule, always check with the airlines in advance of your flight to see what is available. If you must have special food or you're on a restricted diet, consider carrying food onboard your flight.

Cathay Pacific aircraft are equipped with onboard toasters, cappuccino makers, rice cookers and skillets!

In-flight food service has suffered in recent years due to intense cost-cutting with food and beverage among the first items to be slashed, so don't expect anything, even if you're flying first class. In some cases, food is available during the flight, but only for an additional fee.

Some domestic airlines provide no food service (snacks or a meal) on some or all of their flights, while others offer limited and no-frills options. In an attempt to differentiate themselves, some full-service carriers, like British Airways, actually showcase their in-flight food service by enlisting famous chefs to create special menus. Be sure to check out airline profiles to see what popular airlines offer on board.

Singapore Airlines spends about $700 million on food every year and $16 million on wine alone. First class passengers consume 20,000 bottles of alcohol every month and Singapore Airlines is the second largest buyer of champagne in the world.

But how exactly does the food end up in your mouth?

First, the airlines figure out what they need and put it out in a specifications sheet. That information is distributed to food manufacturers.

Then food manufacturers prepare a presentation for them with prototype meals that are made in their test kitchens. Every airline has different requirements.

Let's say the airline likes what a company has to offer. They'll probably go back and forth for awhile until they get exactly what they want. Finally, a contract will be awarded. It's usually 12 to 24 months in length.

Once a company wins the bid, they have to figure out how to turn the prototype meal into a full production meal. That can require small or large tweaks to make sure the product is consistently good when it's mass-produced.

Sometimes, airlines will contract with celebrity chefs to design meals for them. And even though the meals are designed by a celebrity chef, they certainly aren't made by them. The thousands of meals served each day are prepared at a company away from the airport.

Featured on an American Airlines packet of peanuts:
"Instructions: Open packet, eat nuts."

A company does all their manufacturing in a certain facility. From there, a distributor comes to pick up the chow and distribute it. A single company may provide food to airlines throughout the US and Canada, so multiple distributors will end up being used.

The distributor will take the food to the caterer in each airport location. These caterers are the ones you may know – GateGourmet, LSG Sky Chefs, etc. The food manufacturers only makes entrees, so the caterers at the airport take them and add the salad, dinner roll, trays, condiments, etc. They then load the airplane galleys up with food.

American Airlines saved $40,000 in 1987 by removing 1 olive from each
salad served in first class!

This meal is then carried in those little carts to you. Finally, the flight attendant brings the meal to you and you shove it in your mouth – hopefully enjoying it after thinking about its journey to your plate!

So now you know how airlines work. Take a look at the world of airline crews in the next chapter.

Airline Crew: The people that make it all happen

Commercial airplanes are phenomenal pieces of technology, but they're not worth much if you don't have somebody who can fly them! The skills and expertise of pilots are crucial to airline organizations, as well as to getting you where you need to go. The flight-attendant crew is also an important element in the flying process: Attendants try to keep everything running smoothly on each flight, and they deal with the desperate situations that arise when things don't go according to plan.

Now we'll take a look at the fascinating world of airline crews to find out who's working on a typical flight and see what their duties are. The life of an airline crew member can be tiring and frustrating at times, but it is rarely boring. When these people come into work (in an office that cruises a mile or more above the ground), they might very well be headed to the other side of the world.

Although flight crews—pilots and flight attendants—are the most visible occupations, the vast majority of the industry's employees work in ground occupations!

Pilots

Sure, commercial airplanes are modern, but you wouldn't get very far on a flight without pilots: They are the people who put all that sophisticated equipment to work. On commercial airlines, there are always at least two pilots, and on some older aircraft, there are three. All airline pilots have had extensive training and flying experience, often as part of military service. The road from the first training flight to the airline cockpit is a long and difficult one, but for many pilots, this is the only way to go.

On commercial aircraft, two pilots usually make up the cockpit crew. On an airliner, the pilot in command is called the captain. The captain, who generally sits on the left seat in the cockpit, is ultimately responsible for everything that happens on the flight. This includes making major command decisions, leading the crew team, managing emergencies and handling particularly troublesome passengers. The captain also flies the plane for much of the trip, but generally trades off with the first officer at some point. Some pilots I know sometimes trade the seats with their captain or first officer, just to experience sitting in a different seat!

The first officer, the second in command, sits on the right side of the cockpit. He or she has all of the same controls as the captain, and has had the same level of training. The primary reason for having two pilots on every flight is safety. Obviously, if something happens to the captain, a plane must have another pilot who can step in. Additionally, the first officer provides a second opinion on piloting decisions, keeping pilot error to a minimum. Pilots nowadays spend more time on simulators than on real planes. Simulators are important because they give pilots important decision-making skills. Simulator training has drastically reduced accidents and mishaps due to pilot errors.

The captain and the first officer share flying and other duties, such as communicating with air traffic controllers and monitoring the instruments. Some large aircraft have a third crewmember, the flight engineer, who assists the pilots by monitoring and operating many of the instruments and systems, making minor in-flight repairs, and watching for other aircraft.

The flight engineer also assists the pilots with the company, air traffic control, and cabin crew communications. New technology can perform many flight tasks, however, and virtually all new aircraft now fly with only two pilots, who rely more heavily on computerized controls.

A pilot typically arrives at the airport at least an hour before departure (two hours for international flights). Most airlines have a computerized check-in system in the pilot's lounge. This gives the pilots the details of the flight, including the weather, the number of passengers on board and the other crew members who will be working. In order to keep everything in one place, pilots generally keep their flight papers and any other information in a large briefcase. In the time before takeoff, a pilot reviews this information, works out the flight plan, files it with air traffic control and meets with the rest of the crew.

Pilots perform their pre-flight checks before pushing back from the gate.

Before departure, pilots plan their flights carefully. They thoroughly check their aircraft to make sure that the engines, controls, instruments, and other systems are functioning properly. They also make sure that baggage or cargo has been loaded correctly. They confer with flight dispatchers and aviation weather forecasters to find out about weather conditions en route and at their destination.

Based on this information, they choose a route, altitude, and speed that will provide the safest, most economical, and smoothest flight. When flying under instrument flight rules—procedures governing the operation of the aircraft when there is poor visibility—the pilot in command, or the company dispatcher, normally files an instrument flight plan with air traffic control so that the flight can be coordinated with other air traffic.

Takeoff and landing are the most difficult and dangerous parts of the flight, and require close coordination between the two pilots. For example, as the plane accelerates for takeoff, the pilot concentrates on the runway while the copilot, scans the instrument panel. To calculate the speed they must attain to become airborne, pilots consider the altitude of the airport, outside temperature, weight of the plane, and speed and direction of the wind. The moment the plane reaches takeoff speed, one pilot informs the other, and they then pull back on the controls to raise the nose of the plane. Captains and first officers usually alternate flying each leg from takeoff to landing.

The only thing worse than a captain who has never flown as a copilot is a copilot who was once a captain.

Before leaving the gate, the captain must sign the flight release - a document attesting that the crew is fit and that the pilots have reviewed the flight information. While they're preparing for takeoff, the pilots will receive an up-to-date weather report and passenger count and a pre-departure clearance form. To make the paperwork easier, many airplane cockpits are equipped with a built-in printer that receives information from the gate agents and the control tower.

When the paperwork is finished, the attendants secure all the doors and the captain gives the go-ahead for "pushback" (pushing the plane back from the gate so it can move onto the runway). Then, the pilots simply wait their turn and follow 's instructions for takeoff.

Unless the weather is bad, the flight goes routine. Airplane pilots, with the assistance of autopilot and the flight management computer, steer the plane along their planned route and are monitored by the air traffic control stations they pass along the way. They regularly scan the instrument panel to check their fuel supply; the condition of their engines; and the air-conditioning, hydraulics, and other systems.

In an emergency, of course, things can get a lot more hectic. All airline pilots have extensive training in dealing with the unexpected and keeping a cool head in

"There's no such thing as a natural-born pilot."
— Chuck Yeager

precarious situations. Fortunately, it is only on rare occasions that pilots have to put this training to work, but they must be ready to leap into action at all times.

Pilots may request a change in altitude or route if circumstances dictate. For example, if the ride is rougher than expected, pilots may ask air traffic control if pilots flying at other altitudes have reported better conditions; if so, they may request an altitude change. This procedure also may be used to find a stronger tailwind or a weaker headwind to save fuel and increase speed.

Flying does not involve physical work. However, pilots can feel a lot of stress because they know that they are responsible for the safety of their passengers. They must be careful and quick to react if something goes wrong. Many pilots have saved the lives of passengers by quick thinking and reaction.

For example, Chelsey Sullenberger, captain of US Airways Flight 1549, successfully landed his aircraft in the Hudson River after his engines went out due to a bird strike. He later said about how they landed the plane, "It was very quiet as we worked, my co-pilot and I. We were a team. But to have zero thrust coming out of those engines was shocking—the silence." After the airplane landed on the river, Sullenberger even walked the length of the passenger cabin twice to make sure everyone had evacuated before retrieving the plane's maintenance logbook and being the last to evacuate the aircraft. This explains how calm and composed pilots are trained to be even during an emergency.

The successful pilot must have a quick eye and steady nerves.
— W. J. Abbot

Both pilots in the flight crew have equal levels of training, but they usually have varying degrees of seniority. At most airlines, the career track is based almost completely on length of service. To become a captain, you have to rise through the ranks and wait until it's your turn and a position opens up. Seniority also dictates the sorts of planes a pilot flies, as well as his or her schedule. Pilots who are relatively new to the airline will fly reserve, meaning they do not have a set flying schedule.

A reserve pilot may have "on call" duty for 12 hours or longer at a stretch. In this time, the pilot has to be packed and ready to fly, because the flight scheduler might page them at any moment. If a pilot is called in, he or she reports to the airport immediately for a flight assignment (for many airlines, the pilot must be ready to go within an hour of being paged). Reserve pilots are called up when the scheduled pilot becomes ill or can't make the flight for some other reason.

The life of the reserve pilot is largely unpredictable: Pilots might spend several days on reserve and never get paged, or they might get paged every day. And when they report for duty, they could be flying over to the next state or they might be putting in a three-day trip to another part of the world. With this hectic schedule, it's no wonder flights are occasionally delayed while waiting around for crew members to arrive.

The three most common phrases used by pilots are "Was that for us?" "What'd he say?" and "Oh Shit!" Since computers were involved in flying, a new phrase has been added: "What's it doing now?"

Pilots with more seniority pick out a regular flight schedule, called a line. Pilots holding a line live a more "ordinary" sort of life, in the sense that they know ahead of time when they'll be working. But even these pilots spend a lot of time away from their families, and they never know what delays they'll encounter.

So now you know what pilots do.

Language of the Skies

For many pilots, flight training also includes language lessons. Pilots fly all over the world, and to do their job correctly, they must communicate with local air traffic controllers wherever they go. The only way for the system to work properly is if everybody involved can speak the same language.

International treaties have designated English as the official language for airplane communication, though airports may use another language if both the pilot and the controller can speak it. The controllers must speak in English if the flight crew is not comfortable speaking the native language.

Unfortunately, many pilots only learn enough English to get by, leading to occasional misunderstandings. One Avianca airlines jet crashed near New York because they reported their low fuel as a 'priority' and not as an 'emergency'.

It's not clear how many accidents and incidents are the results of language barriers, but some studies show that the problem is getting worse. In the future, new international agreements may establish testing and training standards to assure that all airline pilots can actually speak adequate English.

Passengers prefer old captains and young flight attendants.

Flight Attendants

Major airlines are required by law to provide flight attendants for the safety and security of the traveling public. Although the primary job of the flight attendants is to ensure that security and safety regulations are followed, attendants also try to make flights comfortable and enjoyable for passengers.

In most countries, it is a requirement that there must be at least one flight attendant for every 50 seats in an aircraft. These attendants have a variety of responsibilities in their work, which begins before the first passenger boards and continues through the entire flight. At least 1 hour before takeoff, attendants are briefed by the captain—the pilot in command—on such things as emergency evacuation procedures, coordination of the crew, the length of the flight, expected weather conditions, and any special issues having to do with passengers. Before the plane takes off, the attendants must:

- Greet passengers
- Check their boarding passes
- Direct them to their seats
- Help passengers stow their carry-on luggage
- Make sure passengers near the emergency exits are prepared to help out in an emergency
- Run over safety procedures or show a safety video
- Check every seat to make sure all passengers are buckled-in and their seats are in the correct position.
- Lock the doors and arm them so that the emergency slides will inflate if they are opened
- Check that an adequate supply of food and beverages is available onboard.

After they have worked through this checklist, flight attendants strap themselves into their jump seats. Once the plane levels off, the attendants prepare food and drinks, load the refreshment and meal carts, and serve the passengers.

Lead flight attendants, also known as pursers, oversee the work of the other attendants aboard the aircraft, while performing most of the same duties.

Additionally, attendants must make sure that all passengers adhere to the safety guidelines, and they have to deal with any emergency situations that come up. If there is a problem with the plane, the crew must keep the passengers calm and help them exit the aircraft if necessary. Attendants must also be prepared to deal with terrorists, irate passengers and various medical emergencies. In situations where most people would be paralyzed with panic, flight attendants have to keep their wits about them and work through the emergency.

To deal with all of these duties, a flight attendant must possess certain abilities and personality traits. Airlines look for friendly people who can memorize a lot of information and keep a cool head under pressure. To get a position with an airline, potential flight attendants must interview for the job, pass a medical exam, and work their way through a rigorous schedule of instruction and performance reviews. Flight attendants are normally trained in the hub or headquarters city of an airline over a period that may run from six weeks to six months, depending on the country and airline.

A potential attendant lives with other candidates at a hotel or dorm facility, where they attend classes on everything from food service to dealing with armed hijackers. However, the main focus of training is safety. At this time, the candidates may receive a weekly allowance for expenses, but they aren't actually considered airline employees. They are not hired officially until after they complete the entire training course and pass all tests.

"Air Stewardess" was the official title given to the position that we now refer to as "flight attendant". The first Air Stewardess was Ellen Church and she began work with United Airlines in May 1930.

There are many more flight-attendant applicants than there are flight-attendant positions, so only a select few make it through the entire process and get hired by the airline. The position is competitive primarily because of the unique benefits it offers. In most airlines, flight attendants can fly domestically and internationally at minimal cost as long as the plane has available seats. People are also attracted to flight-attendant work because it doesn't have a five-day, "9-to-5" schedule.

As with pilots, a flight attendant's work schedule is determined by seniority. Newer flight attendants have to fly reserve, rarely knowing where they will be headed the next day. They are at the mercy of the crew-schedulers - the airline employees who figure out who needs to be where on a day-to-day basis. After a year, or in some cases many years, attendants may hold their own line, maintaining a regular, set schedule.
The world of flight attendants and pilots has changed considerably since the beginning of commercial aviation.

The friendliest stewardesses are those on the trip home.
— **cliché**

Airline Crew History

Since the very first airplanes, pilots have been the stars of the aviation world, though their role has evolved considerably over the years. The major developments in the world of pilots have been due to new equipment and changing training standards. When airplanes were first invented, they had a relatively simple control system and were often piloted by the designers themselves. Flying was a difficult skill, but since absolutely everybody was an amateur, the only way to pick it up was by trial and error.

As airplane technology advanced, more and more training was required. Automated systems and sophisticated instruments did a lot of the flying work for the pilot, but the pilot also had to understand what everything did. Pilots have to go through a lot of work before they can fly for the major airlines.

The first widespread, standardized pilot training came during World War I, when militaries started to put soldiers up in the air. Military aircraft training was expanded during World War II and the following decades.

In the 1920s, the U.S. began regulating both aircraft design and pilot training, and the only practical way to meet airline standards was to have extensive military flying experience. In the 1930s through the 1960s, the vast majority of airline pilots in the United States were white men with some military background. Today, there are more and more women and minority pilots, and roughly half of all current U.S. airline pilots were never in the military.

The world of flight attendants has also changed significantly since the beginning of commercial air travel. The first airliners were actually mail planes with a few extra spaces for passengers. On these flights, you had to take care of yourself: The plane crew included only pilots and they were so busy flying the plane that they didn't have time to attend to passengers.

Eventually, some early airlines added cabin boys to their flights. These crew members, who were usually teenagers or small men, were mainly on board to load luggage, reassure nervous passengers and help people get around the plane. In 1930, a young nurse named Ellen Church, along with Steve Stimpson of Boeing Air Transport, came up with a new sort of attendant. Church proposed that registered nurses would make an ideal addition to the flight crew, as they could take care of any passengers that got sick. Boeing, then an airline as well as a plane manufacturer, hired eight nurses for a three-month trial run. The new attendants, who would come to be called "stewardesses," soon, became an integral part of the airline industry. In time, these attendants were no longer required to have a nursing degree, but the nurturing, maternal character remained a key element in the profession.

Until relatively recently, airline stewardesses were under strict control. They were not allowed to be married -- ostensibly because husbands would complain that the long hours kept their wives away from home -- and most airlines had certain constraints on their height, weight and proportions. Their clothing was similarly restrictive: At most airlines, stewardesses wore form-fitting uniforms and were required to wear white gloves and high heels throughout most of the flight. While it was a perfectly respectable occupation for young women, early stewardesses were generally underpaid, had minimal benefits and were in a subservient role to pilots.

The first women flight attendants in 1930 were required to weigh no more than 115 pounds, be nurses, and unmarried.

The early stewardesses had capes that suggested the nursing profession, but also had deep pockets for vital items. Each stewardess had a screwdriver (important to bolt down seats), chewing gum, and railroad timetables. All too often engine trouble or bad weather would force an airplane down. It was the duty of the stewardess to use the railroad table to try to find the now-stranded passengers a connecting train to complete his or her journey. Some other duties were punching tickets, tagging bags and even swatting flies in the cabin after takeoff!

During the 1960s, '70s and '80s, flight-attendant unions, as well as representatives from the equal rights movement, brought about sweeping changes in the airline industry that addressed these problems. Since the 1970s, the policy of the major airlines has been to hire both men and women as attendants and to have no restrictions on size and weight. Flight attendants now share many of the same benefits as pilots, and airlines recognize them as a crucial component of the air-travel industry. After all, to most passengers, the flight attendant is the face of the entire airline.

As the airline industry continues to expand to meet growing consumer demand, more and more young people are joining airline crews. To those workers who can stand the long hours and unpredictable lifestyle, there's nothing quite like flying through the air for a living.

Now you know how pilots and flight attendants keep you comfortable in the sky. Next, take a look at where your bag goes after it disappears through the conveyer belt.

Baggage Handling: Where is my bag?

When you arrive at an airport and check your bags in, have you ever wondered where they go? In this chapter, we'll take a look at the entire process of baggage handling - from checking your bag in to collecting it at baggage claim.

Passengers with their baggage at the check-in desk

The baggage handling system at an airport plays a crucial role in keeping travelers happy. It can also make the difference in an airport's ability to attract or keep a major airline hub. Baggage handling at the airport is a series

of some crucial steps laden with some high-tech devices. The system has to be well-managed in order to keep the travelers happy and satisfied with the service. This cannot be achieved without conveyers, automatic scanners or destination-coded vehicles (DCV). There is an obvious indication of a successful baggage handling system - check if the bags are moving at the same pace as the traveler or not. In case the luggage is traveling slower than the owner, then this will create a lot of frustration for people as they have to wait too long for their bags. This can get even worse if the luggage misses the connecting flight on time.

In the opposite scenario, if the bags move too fast, then again there would be frustration on the travelers end. There is a likelihood that the luggage makes it to the connecting flight but the passenger misses it. Therefore, there must be a sufficient balance to prevent this from happening. The baggage handling system basically has three tasks that it has to accomplish accordingly.
    1. Transfer luggage from check-in area to departure gate
    2. Shift the bags from one gate to another while transferring
    3. Transfer the bags from the arrival gate to the baggage-claim counter

For the remaining part of time when you are at the airport, the luggage stays with you. However, the point that every airport has its own requirements cannot be ignored. The time taken by the passenger to move from check-in area to the gate can vary in different airports. For some airports it is just a walk where others, the passengers may have to take a train. The luggage of the passenger travels according to the time taken by the passenger to reach the appropriate terminal.

59% of people check-in through the airline's main counter, which takes an average of 19 minutes.

Baggage Handling Basics

A baggage handling system can rightly be compared to a road system in a city in which case the conveyers are the local roads, DCV tracks are highways and your bags are of course the vehicles. In a road system, vehicles have the freedom to decide where they are going. However, unlike a road system, the baggage handling system at the airport makes the decision as to where your bag will be going. Baggage-handling and road systems share these properties:

- If a conveyor or DCV track is blocked (a traffic jam, of sorts), baggage can be routed around the blockage.
- Baggage starts and ends its journey on conveyors (just as you start your drive to work on local roads), moving to the DCV track to make longer journeys, such as from terminal to terminal or gate to gate.
- The DCVs never stop, just as there are no stop lights on a highway.

Unlike a road system, however, a baggage-handling system makes all of the decisions about where a bag is going. Hundreds of computers keep track of the location of every bag, every traveler's itinerary and the schedules of all the planes. Computers control the conveyor junctions and switches in the DCV tracks to make sure each bag ends up exactly where it needs to go. Denver Intl. Airport has "more than 19 miles (30 km) of DCV track, more than 5 miles (8 km) of conveyors, 4,000 DCVs, enabling it to handle over 1,000 bags per minute", HowStuffWorks.com notes.

The process begins when you check in and hand your bag to the agent.

Baggage Check-in

When you check in, the agent pulls up your itinerary on the computer and prints out one or more tags to attach to each of your pieces of luggage. The tag has all of your flight information on it, including your destination and any stopover cities, as well as a bar code that contains a ten-digit number.

> 18% of people use a self-check-in kiosk to check their baggage in, which averages 8 minutes.

This number is unique to your luggage. All of the computers in the baggage-handling system can use this number to look up your itinerary.

Your bag's first stop (after check-in) is at an automated bar-code scanner. This station is actually an array of bar-code scanners arranged 360 degrees around the conveyor, including underneath. This device is able to scan the bar codes on about 90 percent of the bags that pass by. The rest of the bags are routed to another conveyor to be manually scanned.

Once the baggage-handling system has read the 10-digit bar-code number, it knows where your bag is at all times.

Conveyors take each bag to the appropriate destination. For example, it routes bags headed out of the country through X-ray machines and other security devices.

> 10% people check-in at curbside (airlines charge an extra fee for this), which averages 13 minutes.

Conveyors

The conveyors in the main terminal of any airport comprise a huge network. There are hundreds of different conveyors with junctions connecting all of them. The conveyor system has to sort all of the bags from all of the different airlines and send them to DCVs that are headed to the proper terminal.

Once your bag has been scanned, the baggage-handling system tracks its movement. At any time, it knows exactly where your bag is on the conveyor system. When your bag comes to a junction, a machine called a pusher either lets it pass or pushes it onto another conveyor.

Through this network of conveyors and junctions, your bag can be sent to nearly any destination automatically.

The last step in the main-terminal conveyor system is a conveyor that loads your bag into a passing DCV. This step is the equivalent of a highway on-ramp.

DCVs

The job of the destination-coded vehicle (DCV) is to move your bag quickly to an off-ramp at the gate. DCVs are used at major airports because the distance from the main terminal to the passenger concourses is quite long, and passengers make the commute fairly quickly by train. "The DCV can travel up to five times faster than a conveyor -- almost 20 mph (32 kph)", notes HowStuffWorks.com

The DCV is a metal cart with wheels on the bottom and a plastic tub on top. Its only electronic device is a passive radio-frequency circuit that broadcasts a unique number identifying that particular car. This is similar to the circuit inside anti-shoplifting devices.

The DCV rides on a metal track, like a roller coaster. It is propelled by linear induction motors mounted to the track. Unlike most electric motors, a linear induction motor has no moving parts. It uses electromagnets to build two magnetic fields -- one on the track and one on the bottom of the DCV -- that are attracted to each other. This is similar to the principle that Maglev trains work on. The motor moves the magnetic field on the track, pulling the DCV along behind it at a high rate of speed. The main advantages of this system are its speed, efficiency, durability, precision and manageability.

"A metal plate that hangs down from the bottom of the DCV rides between the linear induction motors. The motors are located about every 50 feet (15 m). Each time a DCV passes through one of the motors, it receives a boost from the motor that allows it to maintain speed while it coasts to the next motor on the track."

Most passengers today obtain their boarding pass for the flight through the Internet.

"The tub on the DCV is mounted on a pivot. Most of the time, the tub is tilted backward so that the bags cannot slide out (remember that DCVs can go around turns at almost 20 mph/32 kph). A linkage on the DCV locks the tub in this position", marks HowStuffWorks.com

When the DCV comes into a loading area, a bar on the track rises and engages a lever on the DCV. This lever tilts the tub into a flat position.

At the moment when an empty DCV is in front of the loading conveyor, your bag leaves the end of the conveyor belt and slides into the tub. This happens without the DCV stopping, so very precise timing is needed. The conveyors have optical pickups so they know exactly where your bag is and can make sure it hits the DCV perfectly each time.

Once your bag is loaded into the DCV, a rail on the track tilts the tub backward. Unloading a DCV is a similar process. A mechanism on the track engages a lever on the DCV that causes the tub to tilt downward and dump your bag onto a section of conveyor that runs alongside the track.

The DCVs unload in one smooth motion as they move past the unload conveyer. After your bag has been deposited, a bar on the track raises the tub back into the tilted position.

By this point, your bag is very close to the plane.

On March 8, 1994, Don Ku was granted a patent for wheeled suitcase with a collapsible towing handle.

Loading the Plane

There is an off-ramp at every gate in the terminal. The bags make their way down a short conveyor to a sorting station on the ground at the gate.

At the sorting station, baggage handlers load the bags onto carts or into special containers that go right into the airplane. When loading the plane, bags that will be making a transfer after the flight are loaded into separate areas than bags that will be heading to baggage claim. A monitor at the sorting station tells the handlers which bags are going where (remember, the baggage-handling system always knows exactly where each bag is going).

After the bags are loaded into carts or containers, they are brought the short distance to the plane and loaded. Some planes are bulk loaded, meaning the bags are brought up one-by-one on a conveyor and placed into shelves in the cargo hold. Other planes are container loaded, meaning that special containers are loaded on the ground and then placed into the plane.

Luggage being loaded onto a waiting plane

Making Transfers

Since many major airports are hubs, most of the people coming through it are making transfers. Again, the goal of the system is to have the bags keep up with the passengers. Generally, the people can get off the plane faster than the bags can be unloaded, so for the bags to keep up they need to be able to move between gates very quickly.

The terminal is long, and some bags may have to travel that whole distance. The terminal has two separate DCV tracks that make loops around the terminal in opposite directions.

The transferring bags are loaded onto conveyors, where they move through scanning stations and then are routed onto the DCV track. The DCV takes the bags to the proper gate and unloads them.

If you're not making a transfer, your bag has to make it to the baggage-claim area.

Baggage Claim

Bags coming off a plane that are staying in a city are loaded into carts and pulled by tug to the baggage-claim area. Since the bags are already sorted when they come off the plane, it is easy to keep the transferring bags separate from the terminating bags.

Baggage claim area at an airport

When the bags get to the baggage-claim area, they are loaded onto a short conveyor that deposits them onto the carousel.

At airports for cities like Denver, which is a popular destination for skiers, there is a whole separate carousel for skis.

Lost Luggage

During this entire journey however, bags do get lost or damaged at times. Lost luggage is the phenomenon in which an airline does not send a passenger's luggage to the correct destination to arrive with the passenger. In the United States, an average of 1 of 150 people have their checked baggage misdirected or left behind each year!

"The thing I miss about Air Force One is they don't lose my luggage."
— President George Bush Sr.

Lost or misdirected luggage becomes more common the more elaborate a flight plan is. International flights or flights with connections are far more likely to see luggage get lost. There are many causes of lost luggage. If a passenger arrives late for a flight, their luggage will sometimes not have enough time to be loaded on the plane. If tags are accidentally torn off by airport workers, they may not know where to send the luggage. Human error is also common as tags are misread or luggage is placed in the wrong location. Sometimes there is no room in the plane or weight problems. Security delays can also cause bags to arrive on a later flight than their owner. Customs processing is normally handled after luggage is picked up.

Most lost luggage is quickly sent by the airline to the correct destination. For the inconvenience airlines will often reimburse passengers for toiletries, clothing, and other essentials if the arrival airport is away from the passenger's home area. In most cases, upon the arrival of delayed luggage, a courier service will deliver it from the arrival airport to the passenger at his or her home or hotel. Delivery charges are paid by the airline except in rare cases.

On some occasions luggage is completely lost and cannot be recovered. The airline will then normally compensate the owner. The passengers must then list the contents of their baggage and file a claim. Most airlines maintain stores where they sell the contents of lost or abandoned luggage. If a bag is never recovered it is usually because it has been stolen or mistaken by another passenger or stolen by an airport employee.

The normal path for a bag is check the bag in, put the bag on the plane, unload the bag at the destination and put the bag on the carousel for passengers to collect. However, as shocking as it might sound, that is not exactly the route taken by hundreds of bags found in a container behind a Houston pet store!

To deal with lost luggage travelers are advised to carry all essentials in a carry-on bag, including a change of clothes and anything they would be greatly troubled to lose because of monetary or emotional value.

Bags can also be damaged during travel, but most damage (such as broken wheels and handles) is not covered under the airlines' contract of carriage. In general airlines regard the purpose of luggage to be the protection of its contents during transit. If the luggage is damaged, even severely, but the contents remain unharmed then airlines regard the luggage as having fulfilled its purpose and will not compensate owners.

So the next time you collect your bag after a flight, pick it up with a smile, remembering its entire journey to get to you.

Luggage carts outside an airport

> *"The scientific theory I like best is that the rings of Saturn are composed entirely of lost airline luggage."*
> **— Mark Russell**

Airports: The home of airlines

Airports are the places from which an airline operates. You've probably been to airports many times - they are so familiar that you may not pay much attention to them anymore. But if you go behind the scenes, airports are amazing "mini-cities," providing different services to all sorts of people and companies. Air travelers, airlines, private pilots and freight carriers all use airports in completely different ways. Why, airports are as amazing as airlines!

In this chapter, we will take a look at airports and why they are important during our travel.

Main terminal of Washington Dulles International Airport

What are airports?

An airport is a facility; buildings, runways, airplane parking stands and car parks all built and maintained so that airlines can fly airplanes in and out of a particular location. This facility enables passengers to get on and off those planes and also for freight to be loaded and unloaded. Aircraft are also refueled, restocked and maintained.

Airport Terminals

The first thing you do when you arrive at the airport is enter the terminal.

An airport terminal is a building at an airport where passengers transfer between ground transportation and the facilities inside the terminal like gates that allow them to board and disembark from aircraft.

Within the terminal, passengers can purchase tickets, check in for a flight, transfer their luggage, and go through security to get to a gate. The buildings that provide access to the airplanes (via gates) are typically called concourses.

Smaller airports have one terminal while larger airports have several terminals and concourses. At small airports, the single terminal building typically serves all of the functions of a terminal and a concourse.

> *I did not fully understand the dread term 'terminal illness' until I saw Heathrow for myself.*
> **— Dennis Potter**

Some larger airports have one terminal that is connected to multiple concourses via walkways, shuttles, automated transport, sky-bridges, or underground tunnels (such as Denver International Airport). Some larger airports have more than one terminal, each with one or more concourses (such as New York's La Guardia Airport). Still other larger airports have multiple terminals each of which incorporates the functions of a concourse (such as Dallas Fort Worth International Airport).

Most airport terminals are built in a plain style. However, some are monumental in stature, while others are considered architectural masterpieces, like some terminals at major airports.

An airport terminal offers passengers various services for their convenience and comfort. Let's take a closer look at them.

Signs inside an airport

Customers and Passengers

Any major airport has lots of customers, most of them passengers. Most of those passengers, either going somewhere or coming from somewhere are going to want to have a snack, use the restroom, rest for a while, buy a magazine, or even shop for clothes!

To meet passengers' needs, an airport must be accessible by roadways and public transportation, plus have plenty of parking.

It should have areas for ticketing, check-in and baggage handling services.

> *...Hell, which as every frequent traveler knows, is in Concourse D of O'Hare Airport.*
> **— Dave Barry (There is no concourse D at O'Hare)**

Airport security is important to keep the passengers safe. To cater to passenger's needs, an airport needs to have cafes, restrooms and other services.
It should also maintain areas for the customs services for people coming and going out of the country.

Airports have other customers to take care of, too - airplanes that fly in and out of the airport. Airlines need space for airplanes, facilities for routine maintenance, jet fuel and places for passengers and flight crews while on the ground which an airport has to provide. Cargo airlines need space for loading and unloading cargo airplanes. Pilots and other crew members need runways, aircraft fuel, air traffic information, facilities for aircraft storage and maintenance and places to relax while on the ground.

Airports have facilities to meet all of these needs. They have runways, ground concourses, terminals, fuel depots, hangars and a control tower, to name a few.

Generally, airport services can be classified as groundside and airside.

Ground Transportation

You need to get to the airport to board a flight. An airport can't exist in isolation. It depends on a massive transportation system so that people can get to and from the airport and get from place to place within the airport structure itself. While your first thought about an airport is air travel, ground transportation is pretty crucial to an airport's operation.

Some transportation methods are
- **Roads** allow access to and from the airport.
- **Parking** allows short and long-term storage of automobiles. Parking can be on or off airport grounds, and some parking systems are run by private vendors under airport regulation.
- **Passenger drop-off and pick-up areas** make it easier for passengers to get into the terminals, although they are often plagued by traffic congestion because so many people are trying to get in and out.
- **Rental car companies** serve airports.
- **Shuttle services** provide passengers with transportation to local hotels and off-site parking facilities.
- **Private transportation** is available in the form of limousines, vans and taxis.
- **Public transportation** (such as municipal buses and subways) may have stations at an airport.
- **Internal subway trains and trams** may be available to help passengers get to the terminal gates from the concourse.

Atlanta Intl Airport is the busiest airport by passenger traffic and number of landings and take-offs since 1999, serving 88 million passengers per year! This airport is so busy, that people say, upon one's death, regardless of whether the person goes to heaven or hell, the person will connect in Atlanta to get there! This airport even has an automated people mover called "The Plane Train".

Concourses and Terminals

Every day, hundreds of thousands of people move through an airport. They need certain services. Airports provide those services in their concourses and terminals, the heart of any airport. There you'll find the space for airlines to handle ticket sales, passenger check-in, baggage handling and claims.

Concourses are the large halls where you'll find shops, restaurants and lounges. Terminals are the long halls lined by the gates where you board and disembark airplanes and enter the airport.

Most of the time, and in most airports, concourse areas are accessible to the general public (passengers and non-passengers). The gate areas are restricted by airport security to ticket-holding passengers only. Generally, airport security and customs lies between the concourse and the gates.

> *In the space age, man will be able to go around the world in two hours — one hour for flying and one hour to get to the airport.*
> **— Neil McElroy, 'Look,' 1958**

We saw in the first chapter that the food that passengers eat while onboard the airplane is usually provided by private companies contracted by one or more airlines at an airport. The food is prepared in a building that is off the airport grounds, shipped to the airport by truck and loaded onto the plane by the catering company's personnel. For example, Sky Chefs is one of the catering contractors at an airport. They prepare and load thousands of meals per day for various airlines.

Airline freight and private air-freight services such as Fed Ex and DHL may have their own terminals at the airport.

Airports with international flights have customs and immigration facilities. However, as some countries have agreements that allow travel between them without customs and immigrations, such facilities are not a definitive need for an international airport. International flights often require a higher level of physical security, although in recent years, many countries have adopted the same level of security for international and domestic travel.

Some airport structures include on-site hotels built within or attached to a terminal building. Airport hotels have grown popular due to their convenience for passengers and easy accessibility to the airport terminal. Many airport hotels also have agreements with airlines to provide overnight lodging for displaced passengers. When I flew Egypt Air, I had a 6 hour stopover at Cairo. They gave me a free stay at a classy hotel close to Cairo airport with a sumptuous lunch.

At Vancouver Airport, depending on their flight, travelers can "pre-clear" U.S. customs and border control inside the airport before flying to the United States and avoid doing this at their destination.

Gates

The gates are where the airplanes park for passenger boarding and deplaning. Passengers wait in the immediate area of each gate to board the plane. Gates are rented by each airline from the airport authority, and some airlines may rent a whole terminal building in their hub airport, in which case the rental fee alone can run into the millions of dollars.

Routine airplane maintenance, such as washing, de-icing and refueling, is done by airline personnel while the plane is parked at the gate. In some cases, other maintenance tasks might be performed at the gate, possibly with passengers onboard the plane -- it is not uncommon to sit on a plane at the gate while maintenance personnel replace something like a hydraulic brake line on an aircraft.

Aerial view of the gates at Seoul Incheon International Airport

Airline baggage handlers load and unload baggage at the gates using baggage trucks and conveyors.

A funny problem that most airports face is that airplanes and their gates are very large compared to people. At some airports there are literally miles of gates. This can mean a whole lot of walking at any big airport.

Runways

When you think about airports as mini-cities, you need to have roads right? Just as connector roads that lead to the freeway or highway, taxiways connect the gates to the runways. Runways are the most important part of the airport, because that is the area where aircraft takeoff and land. Runways are amazing- a typical one is about 2 miles long, as wide as a 16-lane highway and about 3 feet thick!

Think about this: A fully-loaded Boeing 777 or 747-400 weighs about 850,000 pounds. Imagine a rough landing where 850,000 pounds slams down hard onto the runway. Runways have to be specially constructed to take that strain without cracking or, worse, buckling. As they're designing runways, engineers have to consider the number of wheels an airplane has, how far apart those wheels are and the size of the tires. As planes get bigger and bigger, runways have to be re-built to accommodate the increased stresses.

The airport runway is the most important mainstreet in any town.

— Norm Crabtree, former aviation director for the state of Ohio

Main runways are usually oriented to line up with the prevailing wind patterns so that airplanes can take-off into the wind and land with it. Local and ground air traffic controllers determine which runways are used for take-off and which for landing, taking into account weather, wind and air-traffic conditions. In some airports, main runways cross each other, so the controllers have to pay even closer attention.

Planes use taxiways to get from the gate to a main runway for take-off and from a main runway to the gate after landing. Ground controllers direct ground traffic from the airport's tower. Airline ground personnel assist with the push-back and arrival of aircraft in the gate areas, driving the tugs that push the aircraft back and directing traffic with glowing wands.

Airport Codes

Next to a standard name, almost every single airport has two codes, one IATA and one ICAO code. The IATA (International Air Transport Association) code is a three-letter code that is not too hard to link with the airport name itself. For example, the code BRU stands for Brussels Airport (Belgium).

However, the ICAO (International Civil Aviation Organization) code is much more important when it comes to air traffic control. The ICAO code of an airport consists of 4 letters, that all have a special meaning. The first letter refers to the geographical zone the airport is located in, such as an E for Northern Europe, K for the US, F for Southern Africa, etc. The second letter refers to the country, and is usually the first letter of that country. And last but not least, the third and fourth letters refer to the airport itself. Let's take a look at the Brussels Airport example again. The ICAO code of Brussels Airport is EBBR. The E stands for Northern Europe, the B for Belgium and the BR for Brussels. These codes are always used by pilots and air traffic controllers over the radio and are much lesser known by the public.

Airport Lights

Anyone flying into an airport at night sees a multitude of lights in many different colors. Most people understand that the lights help pilots and airport workers to visualize the airport layout, but how do they all work together, and what do the different colors mean?

Airfield lighting systems aren't the same everywhere. A large commercial airport has many different lighting systems to indicate the airport layout and to help guide pilots on approach. A small airfield may have simple lighting to outline the edges, and some very small private airfields have no night lighting at all. However, where lighting is available, the use of that lighting and the colors used are consistent.

Runway Lights

Runway edge lights are raised white lights that outline each side of a runway for its full length. On a large commercial airfield, the color may change to yellow on the last 2000 feet of the runway.

Runway centerline lights are white lights embedded into the runway centerline at large airports. For the last 3,000 feet of runway, the lights alternate between white and red for 2,000 feet and just red for the final 1,000 feet.

Runway end identifier lights are flashing white lights, one on each side of the runway threshold, to give positive indication of the approach end of a runway.

Runway touchdown zone lights are also used at large airports. These are white light bars embedded into the runway on either side of the centerline. They extend from 100 feet past the runway threshold to either 3,000 feet or to the midpoint of the runway, whichever is less.

Airport runway lights at night

Taxiway centerline lead-off and lead-on lights are alternating green and yellow lights leading from the runway centerline to the taxiway. These lights offer visual direction to pilots leaving or entering the runway.

The shortest airport runway with regular Boeing 747 landings and take offs is located at Princess Juliana International Airport in St. Maarten, The Caribbean, which is only 2180 meters long compared to runways at New York's John F Kennedy International Airport, which are more than 2800 meters long.

Land and hold short lights are sometimes used on airfields with runways that intersect. Smaller aircraft that are capable of landing and stopping before the intersection, otherwise known as "holding short" may be given permission to do so. A line of flashing white lights indicates the hold short line.

Fuel

You cannot fly an airplane without fuel. Airplanes almost always have to refuel between flights, and jets love fuel. A 747 can consume up to a gallon (4 liters) of fuel per second, and "filling up the tanks" takes tens of thousands of gallons of fuel. This huge appetite means that a busy airport can sell millions of gallons of gas every day. At many airports, fuel comes into the fuel-storage depot through a pipeline. The depot can also receive fuel from tanker trucks. The fuel is stored in three unloading islands, each with six, 3,000,000-gallon storage tanks, a meter station and dedicated pump that can handle 300 gallons per minute.

At some airports, fuel trucks carry fuel from the storage depot to the airplane for refueling. In others, fuel is pumped through underground pipes directly to the terminals.

Airport Management

Most of the world's airports are owned by local, regional, or national government bodies who then lease the airport to private corporations who oversee the airport's operation. For example, BAA Limited operates seven of the commercial airports in the United Kingdom, as well as several other airports outside of the UK. In India, airports are managed by Airports Authority of India.

In the United States and Canada, commercial airports are generally operated directly by government entities or government-created airport authorities (also known as port authorities).

Airports are huge businesses. For example, you saw that a big airport can have over a hundred acres of floor space in the terminals, millions of cubic yards of concrete in the runways and hundreds of people staffing the facilities.

> *If God had really intended men to fly, He'd make it easier to get to the airport.*
> *— George Winters*

Commercial airports are publicly owned and generally financed through municipal bonds. Airports typically own all of their facilities and make money by leasing them to airlines, air-freight companies and retail shops and services, as well as by charging for services like fuel and parking and through fees and taxes on airline tickets. The revenues pay off the municipal debt and cover the operating costs. Airports often require other sources of funding as well, such as airport bonds and government grants. But most airports are self-sustaining businesses once they become operational.

About 90 percent of employees at airports work for private companies, such as airlines, contractors and concessions. The remaining 10 percent work directly for the airport as administrators, terminal and ground maintenance personnel and safety crews. Air traffic controllers are employees of the federal government. Airports have their own departments of finance, personnel, administration and public relations, much like any city or municipality. They even have a separate department to grant permission for filming at an airport.

Airports with regularly scheduled flights are regulated by the Federal Aviation Administration (FAA) and must also follow local and state government regulations.

Safety

Air safety is an important concern in the operation of an airport, and almost every airfield includes equipment and procedures for handling emergency situations. Commercial airfields include one or more emergency vehicles and their crew that are specially equipped for dealing with airfield accidents, crew and passenger extractions, and the hazards of highly flammable aviation fuel. The crews are also trained to deal with situations such as bomb threats, hijacking, and terrorist activities.

The devil himself had probably redesigned Hell in the light of information he had gained from observing airport layouts.
— Anthony Price, The Memory Trap, 1989

Hazards to aircraft include debris, nesting birds, and reduced friction levels due to environmental conditions such as ice, snow, or rain. In adverse weather conditions, ice and snow clearing equipment can be used to improve traction on the landing strip. For waiting aircraft, equipment is used to spray special deicing fluids on the wings.

Many airports are built near open fields or wetlands. These tend to attract bird populations, which can pose a hazard to aircraft in the form of bird strikes.

Airports have their own crews to handle fire and emergency medical services (EMS). An airport may have several fire/EMS stations on the ground because the Federal Aviation Administration (FAA) requires that emergency crews be able to reach the midpoint of a runway within 3 to 5 minutes. These crews are usually employees of the city or municipality and are stationed at the airport.

Airports also have their own police crews. Some airport police are members of the city or municipality assigned to the airport, while others are from private security companies contracted to patrol the airport grounds (such as the perimeter fences that limit access to the airfield) and to operate the security inspection points within the terminals. Finally, airports must have crews for collecting and disposing trash, keeping terminals clean (some janitorial services are run by airlines or airline cooperatives) and keeping runways clear during foul weather.

For example, without snow-removal crews, aircraft would be grounded whenever a storm hit.

Airports and the environment

Aircraft noise is major cause of noise disturbance to residents living near airports. Sleep can be affected if the airports operate night and early morning flights. Aircraft noise not only occurs from take-off and landings, but also ground operations including maintenance and testing of aircraft. Other noise and environmental concerns are vehicle traffic causing noise and pollution on roads leading the airport. Concorde, the world's first supersonic jet caused a lot of noise disturbance because it flew above the sound barrier.

The construction of new airports or addition of runways to existing airports is often resisted by local residents because of the effect on countryside, historical sites and local plants. Due to the risk of collision between birds and airplanes, large airports undertake population control programs where they frighten or shoot birds.

> *It can hardly be a coincidence that no language on Earth has ever produced the phrase, 'as pretty as an airport.' Airports are ugly. Some are very ugly. Some attain a degree of ugliness that can only be the result of a special effort.*
>
> **— Douglas Adams, The Long Dark Tea-Time of the Soul, 1988**

The construction of airports has been known to change local weather patterns. For example, because they often flatten out large areas, they can be susceptible to fog in areas where fog rarely forms. In addition, they generally replace trees and grass with pavement.

Some of the airport administrations prepare and publish annual environmental reports in order to show how they consider these environmental concerns in airport management issues and how they protect environment from airport operations. These reports contain all environmental protection measures performed by airport administration in terms of water, air, soil and noise pollution, resource conservation and protection of natural life around the airport.

Aerial view of Zurich International Airport

So these are how those mini-cities called airports work. Take a behind-the-scenes tour of what happens when you fly in the next chapter.

What happens when you fly

What happens when you fly on an airplane? You board the aircraft, get into your seat, have a meal, watch a movie, sleep, and get up at your destination. In this chapter, find out what really happens during a commercial airplane flight.

Before takeoff

Long before passengers arrive at the airport, airline maintenance professionals work behind the scenes to ensure aircraft safety, and flight operations dispatchers prepare and adjust flight plans. While the aircraft is secured, passengers and baggage arrive at the airport for screening. The cabin crew and pilots perform a series of checks and briefings to ensure that everything is in order for a safe and secure flight. Later, flight attendants assist passengers to board and stow their luggage, and the pilots follow the procedures and checklists for a safe departure.

Aircraft maintenance

Every day, licensed Aircraft Maintenance Engineers (AMEs) perform a series of tasks from an approved maintenance program to ensure the continued safety of the aircraft. These tasks include checking the tire pressures and inspecting for fluid leaks and damage to aircraft structure, as well as testing the function of systems and controls. If any faults are detected, AMEs take the necessary actions to restore the aircraft to a safe condition for flight.

Flight planning

Hours before takeoff, flight dispatchers prepare the flight plan, a complete review of the route, altitudes, fuel burn and weather conditions for the flight, which also includes detailed information about en route airports, the aircraft and more. Weather patterns are a primary concern in preparing a flight plan, since the pilot needs to avoid such conditions as ice buildup; thunderstorms, windshear and even volcanic ash (remember the Iceland volcanic eruption of 2010?)

Securing the Aircraft

Customer service agents, baggage handlers, and maintenance workers secure aircraft doors, hatches, and passenger bridges, and prevent unauthorized people from accessing the aircraft cabin and cargo compartments. Only authorized security-screened checked-baggage and cargo is loaded onto the aircraft.

Ground Preparations

Ground crews empty the lavatories and fill up the water reservoirs on the aircraft. The amount of fuel designated in the flight plan is carried in a fuel truck to the aircraft and added to the fuel tanks through a hose connected to the aircraft.

Ground preparations are an essential part of any flight and start before the passengers even arrive at the airport

Passenger Screening

Officers screen passengers and their baggage for prohibited or dangerous items before boarding.

Air carriers sometimes implement their own measures to screen passengers against government and internal security watch lists. This includes verifying passengers' identities and matching it to their boarding passes prior to boarding. El Al, supposedly the safest airline in the world, implements strict security measures to protect their flights. They have strict security protocols ranging from full body scans to long interrogations.

Crew Briefing

Cabin crew and pilots meet for a full-crew briefing to prepare for the flight. Interestingly, at some major airlines, cabin crew does not meet each other on or before the day of the flight. However, at some regional airlines, the crew knows each other and flies together often.

Cockpit preparations

When the pilots arrive in the cockpit, they enter their flight plan into a computerized navigation system, perform a number of cockpit safety checks, and prepare for the flight. The captain and first officer run through their emergency responsibilities together.

The very existence of aviation is proof that man, given the will, has the capacity to accomplish deeds that seem impossible.

— Eddie Rickenbacker

Safety Checks

The cabin crew performs checks on all safety equipment in the cabin, as well as an aircraft security check prior to passenger boarding. Food and beverages are brought on to the aircraft by the caterer at this time.

Pre-Boarding

Flight Attendants perform Pre-Boarding of all passengers who have small children or require special assistance and provide these passengers with individual safety briefings if required, and on some airlines, boarding for first and business class passengers.

Boarding Gates at Cape Town International Airport

General Boarding

All the remaining passengers board at this time. As passengers board, they are required to stow their carry-on baggage, including purses, under their seats so that the aircraft can takeoff safely. It is also crucial that passengers turn off their cell phones to prevent causing interference that could put the takeoff at risk.

Cell phones and airplanes

It's a fact of life for every frequent flier: before the plane is off the ground, cell phones must be turned off and put away.
That's the rule and every commercial airline in the United States enforces it. But is there a good reason for this? Can a cell phone bring down a plane, or is that just a myth? The answer is unclear.

Theoretically, it is possible for a cell phone to interfere with airplane navigation systems. How exactly does this interference occur? The interference happens because emissions from electronics can be picked up by other electronics. For example, if there were an electronic device producing emissions in the same band as the aircraft navigation GPS signals, this would interfere with the GPS's ability to accurately determine the position, heading, etc. of the aircraft. Hence, pilots and aircraft systems could be presented with incorrect information from that GPS, because of the interference. Hence, airlines usually ask that during critical operations such a takeoff and landing, that all electronic devices are powered down.

However, even with the strict regulations, there are between one to four 'illegal' phone calls placed on flights!

Closing the cabin door

Flight Attendants can only close the main cabin door once all baggage is stowed. Did you know that every aircraft is certified based on a physical demonstration that the flight can be evacuated within 90 seconds with half of the doors unserviceable?

Safety Briefing

Flight Attendants perform a Safety Briefing for all passengers. Passengers are provided with Safety Features Cards detailing the specific safety features of the aircraft they are flying on. Both the Safety Briefing and Safety Features Cards follow strict guidelines set out by the country's aviation administrations. Even though it has been proven that paying attention to these briefings saves lives when emergencies occur, many frequent fliers do not pay attention to them.

Push Back and Taxiing

Once the cabin door is closed and armed, the pilots complete their before-start checklist and then release the brake to "push back" from the gate. A tow bar is used to push the aircraft to a location where its engines can be safely started once the pilot has received a clearance to do so. Once the tow bar is disconnected, the pilots wait for another clearance from ground control before they may taxi to their runway for takeoff.

British Airways aircraft during pushback

De-icing

If there is ice or snow on the wing or other critical surfaces of the aircraft, it will impact the aircraft's performance and pose a serious risk to the flight; this must be removed before the aircraft may take off. This may add to the scheduled flight time. Once the aircraft has been sprayed, it must be airborne before the anti-icing fluid loses its effectiveness; otherwise the de-icing will have to be repeated.

"God, look at that thing! That don't seem right, does it? That's not right."

— First Officer Roger Pettit, during takeoff roll, Air Florida Flight 90, 1982. Air Florida flight 90 crashed into the Potomac river because of ice and snow buildup on the wings

Takeoff

After turning onto the runway, pilots complete their before-takeoff checks. They advise Flight Attendants to take their positions, and then wait for takeoff clearance from air traffic control before applying thrust for takeoff. The aircraft then accelerates down the runway for takeoff. Sometimes, when traffic at an airport is light, pilots may complete their before-takeoff checks and also receive their clearance before turning onto the runway. Then, as they are turning, they apply full throttle. This is known as a rolling takeoff. Once the aircraft reaches takeoff speed, the pilots pull the nose up. Then the aircraft climbs to its cruising altitude.

Virgin Atlantic 747 just after takeoff at Manchester International Airport. Notice that the landing gear is still retracting

Air Traffic Control

Once the plane has taken off, the pilot radios the departure air traffic controller. The controller is responsible for maintaining separation between aircraft within a designated airspace sector, and clears the aircraft to ascend to higher altitudes for cruise and descent. Throughout the flight, controllers monitor whether the pilots are complying with routing, speed and separation.

Flexible is much too rigid, in aviation you have to be fluid.

— Verne Jobst

In flight

By this time, you are settled into your seat, reading a magazine. But once you are in the air, the crew has responsibility for the safety and security of the flight and all passengers. However, the crew receives constant information and support throughout the flight from Air Traffic Controllers, Flight Dispatch - which coordinates the needs of the flight crew - and various airspace authorities.

How do you like your coffee, Captain - cream & sugar?'
We are at 30 west, the half-way point between the European & North American continents, & the stewardess in charge of the forward galley is looking after her aircrew during a pause in serving the passengers' meals.

Mach 2. On autopilot, eleven miles high, moving at 23 miles a minute. Nearly twice as high as Mount Everest, faster than a rifle bullet leaving its barrel. The side windows are hot to the touch, from friction of the passing air. Despite the speed we can talk without raising our voices.

"Milk, please, & no sugar".

— Brian Calvert, the opening paragraphs of Flying Concorde, 1982.

Landing the aircraft

Before the aircraft can begin its descent, the pilot at the controls must brief the other pilot on which runway will be used for the landing, and details about the approach and landing procedures to be followed. After this, the pilots complete pre-descent and in-range safety checks. When they receive an approach clearance, the pilots begin the descent. Once again, they must receive a clearance from Air Traffic Control before landing.

Mahan Air Airbus A300 lands at Birmingham International Airport

Arriving at the gate

After touching down, the aircraft taxis to the arrival gate via taxiways, where the engines are shut down. At modern airports like Madrid Bajaras, there are automated displays that show the pilots how far the aircraft is from the parking spot.

As soon as the aircraft is at the gate, the cargo doors are opened so that cargo can be unloaded by the baggage handlers. Cabin crew unlocks and opens the cabin door.

> *There is no excuse for an airplane unless it will fly fast!*
> — *Roscoe Turner*

Arrivals

After the cabin door has opened, passengers are instructed to disembark the aircraft. Upon leaving the aircraft, passengers follow signs to the Arrivals area of the airport where their checked baggage will arrive on the baggage carousel after it is unloaded from the aircraft by airline baggage handlers.

Final Checklists

While the passengers are waiting for their bag to arrive, the pilots complete a final safety checklist after the cabin door has been opened. Once this is complete, they leave the aircraft. It is standard practice for the captain to leave the aircraft last.

> *To invent an airplane is nothing. To build one is something.*
> *To fly is everything.*
> **— Otto Lilienthal**

Resolving Aircraft Faults

Aircraft Maintenance Engineers (AMEs) are alerted by the pilots if any aircraft faults were detected during the flight. The AMEs take whatever actions are required to resolve these faults before the aircraft returns to flight.

Then, you go to your destination from the airport. So now you know what goes on behind the scenes when you fly. Take a look at Air Traffic Control, the complex system that guides pilots in the air, in the next chapter.

Roger that: Air Traffic Control

With air travel booming, there are so many planes flying around. They cannot be directed only by instruments, there has to be a person who talks to them during the flight and gives them instructions. You may not pay much attention to it the next time you fly somewhere, but from the moment your airplane door closes, until the moment it opens again at your destination, the timeliness and safety of your journey are ensured by the air traffic control system.

So how does air traffic control actually work, and how does your plane get safely from point A to point B? The system is a complex combination of radar, computers, radios and waypoints. How do these aircraft keep from colliding with each other? How does air traffic move into and out of an airport or across the country?

The task of ensuring safe operations of commercial and private aircraft falls on air traffic controllers. They must coordinate the movements of thousands of aircraft, keep them at safe distances from each other, direct them during takeoff and landing from airports, direct them around bad weather and ensure that traffic flows smoothly with minimal delays.

When you think about air traffic control, the image of men and women in the tower of an airport probably comes to mind. However, the air traffic control system is much more complex than that. In this chapter, we will see what role air traffic control plays in commercial aviation.

Before Air Traffic Control Towers were developed, pilots avoided other aircraft by a method called "see and be seen".

Airspace and Air Traffic Control

Air traffic is controlled by three main work environments:

Control Tower

The control tower is usually located in the airport. It is responsible for the airplane when it is on the ground. When the airplane is off the ground, the TRACON takes over.

Air traffic control tower at an airport

Let's take a peek into what goes on in control tower. Controllers sit in front of computer screens in a dimly lit room for two hours at a time. The screens are filled with lines and dots; the lines are the highways of the skies and the dots are the aircraft that move along those lines. Each aircraft is traveling at different speeds, altitudes, and directions.

Controllers monitor flight patterns via computer screens and through visual observations. Their responsibility is to taxi all ground vehicles and aircraft to and from the runway.

Control towers have teams that handle various phases of the flight such as preflight, clearance delivery, taxi, take-off and landing.

TRACON

A Terminal Radar Approach Control (TRACON) is an air traffic control facility usually located within the vicinity of a large airport. It is responsible for the aircraft from the time the aircraft is off ground till 10,000 ft during both take-off and landing. Typically, the TRACON controls aircraft within a 50 mile radius of the airport. A TRACON is sometimes called Approach Control or Departure Control in radio transmissions.

Area Control Center

Area control centers are responsible for the airplane when it is above 10,000 feet. Area Control Center (ACC) is commonly referred to as a "Center". In the United States, such a center is also referred to as "Air Route Traffic Control Center" (ARTCC). For example, the United States airspace is divided into 21 zones, and each zone is divided into sectors. Each zone is controlled by an ACC.

In the ACC, Controllers work in large radar rooms (about the size of a warehouse) and their locations may vary; sometimes they're located near an airport, sometimes in a remote location that is central to many airports. These controllers are responsible for airspace that encompasses several states.

Whatever the location or position, a controller constantly monitors and makes split-second decisions on how to maneuver aircraft around each other so that each one stays separated by 1,000 feet. At times, they may be communicating with ten pilots simultaneously.

As an aircraft travels through a given airspace division, it is monitored by the one or more air traffic controllers responsible for that division. The controllers monitor this aircraft and give instructions to the pilots. As an aircraft reaches the boundary of a Center's control area it is "handed off" to the next Area Control Center. The current controller gives the pilots a frequency to tune into. However, aircraft have two radio sets, so they are never caught between frequencies while flying. After the hand-off, the aircraft begins talking to the next controller.

Some pilots of small aircraft fly by vision only (visual flight rules, or VFR). These pilots are not required by the FAA to file flight plans and are not serviced by the mainstream air traffic control system. Pilots of large commercial flights use instruments to fly (instrument flight rules, or IFR), so they can fly in all sorts of weather. They must file flight plans and are serviced by the mainstream air traffic control system.

Phases of flight

To make it easier to visualize a typical flight across air traffic control sections, let's explore the various phases of a commercial airplane flight.

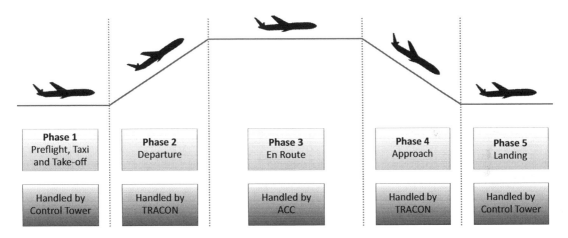

Phases of a commercial flight

Preflight

Before boarding, the pilots lodge a Flight Plan with the Control Tower, providing information about the planned route and destination - all IFR pilots must file a flight plan at least 30 minutes prior to pushing back from the gate. Your pilot reviews the weather along the intended route, maps the route and files the plan. The flight plan includes the airline name and flight number, the aircraft the pilots are flying, the route of the flight, its intended airspeed and its cruising altitude. Your pilot transmits this data to the tower.

> *The more traffic at an airport, the better it is handled.*
> — *cliché*

Clearance Delivery is the process where the Control Tower issues route clearances to aircraft, typically before they commence taxiing. These contain details of the route that the aircraft is expected to fly after departure as mentioned in the preflight section.

Flight Data (which is routinely combined with Clearance Delivery) is the process that is responsible for ensuring that both controllers and pilots have the most current information: pertinent weather changes, outages, airport ground delays/ground stops, runway closures, etc. Flight Data may inform the pilots using a recorded continuous loop on a specific frequency known as the Automatic Terminal Information Service (ATIS). The pilots can tune into this frequency whenever they want this information.

The primary method of controlling the immediate airport environment is visual observation from the control tower. The tower is a tall, windowed structure located on the airport grounds. Tower controllers are responsible for the separation and efficient movement of aircraft and vehicles operating on the taxiways and runways of the airport itself, and aircraft in the air near the airport, generally 2 to 5 nautical miles (4 to 9 km) depending on the airport procedures.

Electronic Flight Strip system at Sao Paolo International Airport

Taxi

The Ground Control team in Control Tower handles most areas of the airport excluding runways. It is responsible for the airport "movement" areas, as well as areas not released to the airlines or other users. This generally includes all taxiways, inactive runways, holding areas, and some intersections where aircraft arrive, having vacated the runway or departure gate. Exact areas and control responsibilities are clearly defined in local documents and agreements at each airport. Any aircraft, vehicle, or person walking or working in these areas is required to have clearance from Ground Control.

Most aircraft and airside vehicles have radios. Aircraft or vehicles without radios must respond to ATC instructions via aviation light signals (more about this later) or else be led by vehicles with radios. People working on the airport surface normally have a communications link through which they can communicate with Ground Control, commonly either by handheld radio or even cell phone. Ground Control is vital to the smooth operation of the airport, because this position impacts the sequencing of departure aircraft, affecting the safety and efficiency of the airport's operation.

China Airlines Cargo 747 taxiing at Manchester International Airport

The ground controller is responsible for all ground traffic, which includes aircraft taxiing from the gates to takeoff runways and from landing runways to the gates. When the ground controller determines that it is safe, he or she directs your pilot to push the plane back from the gate (airline personnel operate the tugs that actually push the aircraft back and direct the plane out of the gate area). As your plane taxis to the runway, the ground controller watches all of the airport's taxiways and uses ground radar to track all of the aircraft (especially useful in bad weather), ensuring that your plane does not cross an active runway or interfere with ground vehicles. The ground controller talks with your pilot by radio and gives him instructions, such as which way to taxi and which runway to go to for takeoff. If radios do not work, then pilots and air traffic control have to rely on Aviation Light Signals.

In the rare case of a radio failure or aircraft not equipped with a radio, air traffic control may use a signal lamp to direct the aircraft. The signal lamp has a focused bright beam and is capable of emitting three different colors: red, white and green. These colors may be flashed or steady, and have different meanings to aircraft in flight or on the ground. Planes can acknowledge the instruction by moving the ailerons if on the ground, or by flashing their landing or navigation lights during hours of darkness.

The similarity between air traffic controllers and pilots?

If a pilot screws up, the pilot dies.

If ATC screws up, the pilot dies.

— cliché

Takeoff

The Tower Control team in the Control Tower is responsible for airplanes on the runways. Tower Control clears aircraft for takeoff or landing, ensuring that prescribed runway separation will exist at all times. If Tower Control detects any unsafe condition, a landing aircraft may be told to "go-around" (missed approach) and be re-sequenced into the landing pattern by the approach or terminal area controller.

Within the airport, a highly disciplined communications process between Tower Control and Ground Control is an absolute necessity. Ground Control must request and gain approval from tower control to cross any active runway with any aircraft or vehicle. Likewise, Tower Control must ensure that Ground Control is aware of any operations that will impact the taxiways, and work with the approach radar controllers to create "holes" or "gaps" in the arrival traffic to allow taxiing traffic to cross runways and to allow departing aircraft to take off.

The tower controller in the tower watches the skies above the airfield and uses surface radar to track aircraft. He or she is responsible for maintaining safe distances between planes as they take off. The tower controller gives your pilot final clearance for takeoff when it is deemed safe, and provides the new radio frequency for the departure controller. At airports with less traffic, tower controllers sometimes give pilots clearance to take-off even before they pull onto the runway. That is why sometimes pilots make a rolling takeoff. However, they also do this while the traffic is high, as air traffic control sometimes hurries them up too. Once clearance is given, your pilot must decide if it is safe to take off. If it is safe, he accelerates the plane down the runway.

As you leave the ground, the tower controller hands your plane off electronically to the departure controller at the TRACON facility that services your departure airport, but still monitors the plane until it is 5 miles from the airport. Your pilot now talks with the departure controller.

Some busier airports have systems designed to display aircraft and vehicles on the ground. These are used by the ground controller as an additional tool to control ground traffic, particularly at night or in poor visibility. There are a wide range of capabilities on these systems as they are being modernized.

Older systems will display a map of the airport and the target. Newer systems include the capability to display higher quality mapping, radar target, data blocks, and safety alerts.

Departure

The phase of flight from the point it takes off the ground till it reaches 10,000 feet altitude is called departure. The departure phase of the flight is handled by the TRACON facility. Once your plane takes off, your pilot activates a transponder device inside the aircraft. The transponder detects incoming radar signals and broadcasts an amplified, encoded radio signal in the direction of the detected radar wave. The transponder signal provides the controller with your aircraft's flight number, altitude, airspeed and destination. A blip representing the airplane appears on the controller's radar screen with this information beside it. The controller can now follow your plane.

The departure control team is located in the TRACON facility, which may have several airports within its airspace (50-mile radius). He or she uses radar to monitor the aircraft and must maintain safe distances between ascending aircraft. The departure controller gives instructions to your pilot (heading, speed, rate of ascent) to follow regular ascent corridors through the TRACON airspace. The departure controller monitors your flight during ascent to the en route portion. When your plane leaves TRACON airspace, the departure controller passes your plane off to the center controller (ACC controller).

En Route

The plane is considered in the en route phase when it is above 10,000 feet altitude. As the airplane enters the en route phase it is handed over by TRACON to the Area Control Center (ACC). Here it is monitored by at least two air traffic controllers. En-route air traffic controllers issue clearances and instructions for airborne aircraft, and pilots are required to comply with these instructions. En-route controllers also provide air traffic control services to many smaller airports around the country, including clearance off of the ground and clearance for approach to an airport. Controllers adhere to a set of separation standards that define the minimum distance allowed between aircraft. These distances vary depending on the equipment and procedures used in providing ATC services.

The radar controller is in charge of all air-to-ground communication, maintains safe separation of aircraft within the sector and coordinates activities with other sectors and/or centers. The controllers must monitor the airspace at high altitude and low altitude. The center controllers provide your pilot with updated weather and air-traffic information. They also give directions to your pilot regarding such aspects as speed and altitude to maintain a safe separation between aircraft within their sector. They monitor your plane until it leaves their sector. Then they pass it off to another sector's controller.

German air traffic controllers, earn an average of about $200,000 a year, British controllers around $160,000. In the United States, the average annual salary was $110,000 in 2009.

Another controller, called the radar hand-off controller, assists the radar and associate radar controllers during times of heavy traffic, watching the radar screen and helping to maintain smooth air-traffic flow.

While you are enjoying your meal, snack, in-flight movie or the view outside the window, your plane passes from sector to sector and gets passed from ACC to ACC. In each sector, center controllers radio instructions to the pilots. The path of your plane may have to be changed from the original flight plan to move around bad weather or avoid a congested sector. Your pilots may request a change in altitude to avoid or reduce turbulence or save fuel. This back and forth between pilots and center controllers continues until you are about 150 miles from your destination. At this point, the center controller directs all planes flying into your destination to move from high altitudes to low altitudes and merges the descending aircraft into a single file line toward the airport. The controller gives instructions to your pilot, such as changes in heading, speed and altitude, to place your plane in line with these other aircraft.

Depending on traffic conditions, the controller may have to place your plane into a holding pattern, which is a standard route around each airport, where you wait until the airport can handle your arrival. The controller continues to give directions to your pilot until your plane is on the approach to landing where it is handed over to TRACON.

> *!FDC 1/9731 FDC SPECIAL NOTICE - DUE TO EXTRADORDINARY CIRCUMSTANCES AND FOR REASONS OF SAFETY. ATTENTION ALL AIRCRAFT OPERATORS, BY ORDER OF THE FEDERAL AVATION COMMAND CENTER, ALL AIRPORTS/ AIRDROMES ARE NOT AUTHORIZED FOR LANDING AND TAKEOFF. ALL TRAFFIC INCLUDING AIRBORNE AIRCRAFT ARE ENCOURAGE TO LAND SHORTLY.*
>
> *— first FDC special notice issued by the FAA on the morning of September 11, 2001, which grounded all U.S. flight operations until further notice after the simultaneous quadruple hijacking. Note that the word "Aviation" was spelled incorrectly.*

Approach

When your descending plane is 50 miles from your destination airport, it handed over to TRACON. An approach controller within the TRACON facility directs your pilot to adjust the aircraft's heading, speed and altitude to line up and prepare to land along standard approach corridors. Your pilot then aligns your plane with the runway. When you are 10 miles from the runway, the approach controller passes your plane off to the tower controller in the airport Control Tower.

Landing

The tower controller in the airport Control Tower checks the runways and the skies above the runways with binoculars and surface radar (tower and ground controllers are the only controllers licensed to use visual information in performing their duties). When the tower controller determines that it is safe, he or she gives your pilot clearance to land. The tower controller also updates weather conditions for your pilot and monitors the spacing between your plane and other landing aircraft.

Iran Air Boeing 747 landing at London Heathrow International Airport

Once you've landed, the tower controller directs your plane to an exit taxiway and tells your pilot the new radio frequency for the ground controller and passes your plane off to the ground controller.

The ground controller watches the runways and taxiways and uses ground radar information to ensure that your taxiing aircraft does not cross active runways or interfere with ground vehicles. He or she directs your plane to the appropriate terminal gate. Ground personnel from the airline use hand signals to assist your pilot in parking the airplane at the gate.

Problems

Every mechanism has its own problems, and air traffic control is no exception. The day-to-day problems faced by the air traffic control system are primarily related to the volume of air traffic demand placed on the system and weather. Several factors dictate the amount of traffic that can land at an airport in a given amount of time. Each landing aircraft must touchdown, slow, and exit the runway before the next crosses the approach end of the runway. This process requires at least one and up to four minutes for each aircraft. Allowing for departures between arrivals, each runway can thus handle about 30 arrivals per hour.

A large airport with two arrival runways can handle about 60 arrivals per hour in good weather. Problems begin when airlines schedule more arrivals into an airport than can be physically handled, or when delays elsewhere cause groups of aircraft that would otherwise be separated in time to arrive simultaneously. Aircraft must then be delayed in the air by holding over specified locations until they may be safely sequenced to the runway.

Up until the 1990s, holding, which has significant environmental and cost implications, was a routine occurrence at many airports. Advances in computers now allow the sequencing of planes hours in advance. Thus, planes may be delayed before they even take off (by being given a "slot"), or may reduce speed in flight and proceed more slowly thus significantly reducing the amount of holding.

Beyond runway capacity issues, weather is a major factor in traffic capacity. Rain, ice or snow on the runway cause landing aircraft to take longer to slow and exit, thus reducing the safe arrival rate and requiring more space between landing aircraft. Fog also requires a decrease in the landing rate. These, in turn, increase airborne delay for holding aircraft. If more aircraft are scheduled than can be safely and efficiently held in the air, a ground delay program may be established, delaying aircraft on the ground before departure due to conditions at the arrival airport.

In Area Control Centers, a major weather problem is thunderstorms, which present a variety of hazards to aircraft. Aircraft will deviate around storms, reducing the capacity of the en-route system by requiring more space per aircraft, or causing congestion as many aircraft try to move through a single hole in a line of thunderstorms. Occasionally weather considerations cause delays to aircraft prior to their departure as routes are closed by thunderstorms.

London Gatwick Airport air traffic control tower

Call Signs

A prerequisite to safe air traffic separation is the assignment and use of distinctive call signs. These are permanently allocated by ICAO on request usually to scheduled flights and some air forces for military flights. They are written callsigns with 3-letter combination like KLM, AAL, SWA, BAW, VLG followed by the flight number, like AAL872, VLG1011. As such they appear on flight plans and ATC radar labels. The callsigns used on the radio contact between pilots and Air Traffic Control are not always identical with the written ones. For example BA stands for British Airways but on the radio you will only hear the word Speedbird instead.

The flight number part is decided by the aircraft operator. In this arrangement, an identical call sign might well be used for the same scheduled journey each day it is operated, even if the departure time varies a little across different days of the week. The call sign of the return flight often differs only by the final digit from the outbound flight. Generally, airline flight numbers are even if eastbound, and odd if westbound. In order to reduce the possibility of two callsigns on one frequency at any time sounding too similar, a number of airlines, particularly in Europe, have started using alphanumeric callsigns that are not based on flight numbers. Additionally it is the right of the air traffic controller to change the 'audio' callsign for the period the flight is in his sector if there is a risk of confusion, usually choosing the tail number instead.

Aircraft call signs will use the suffix "heavy" for heavy aircraft, to indicate an aircraft that is going to cause significant wake turbulence (bumpy air behind it). This "heavy" tag is given to all aircraft that have a takeoff weight of more than 255,000 lbs. The suffix "super" is used for the Airbus A380. For air ambulance services or other flights involving the safety of life (such as aircraft carrying a person who has suffered a heart attack), "lifeguard" is added to the call sign.

Before around 1980, International Air Transport Association (IATA) and ICAO were using the same 2-letter callsigns. Due to the larger number of new airlines after deregulation ICAO established the 3-letter callsigns as mentioned above. The IATA callsigns are currently used in aerodromes on the announcement tables but never used any longer in Air Traffic Control. For example, AA is the IATA callsign for American Airlines — ATC equivalent for AAL. Other examples include LY/ELY for El Al, DL/DAL for Delta Air Lines, VY/VLG for Vueling Airlines, etc.

Air Traffic Control Careers

What does it take to be an air traffic controller? To be a ground controller, you have to memorize the position of aircraft on the runways and taxiways with a single, short glance. Control Tower, TRACON and ACC controllers must be able to think and visualize in three dimensions. All controllers must be able to gather information from what they hear, make decisions quickly and know the geography of their own airspace, as well as that of others. They must be able to read and interpret symbols as well as predict the whereabouts of aircraft from course headings and speeds, and they must be able to concentrate intensely. There has been an incident where an air traffic controller was unaware that a flight was receiving instruction from the on-board automatic Traffic Collision Avoidance System (TCAS) software to climb. He instructed the aircraft to descend and caused a mid-air collision, leading to the deaths of 71 people, including many children. Even though such incidents are rare, they do happen.

In the United States, air traffic controllers at all levels are employed by the FAA. To become an air traffic controller, you must apply through the federal civil-service system and pass a written test that assesses your abilities to perform a controller's duties. Abstract reasoning and 3-D visualization are tested on the exam. Applicants must have three years of work experience, a four-year college degree or some combination of the two.

After graduation, you accumulate work experience at various sites across the country, from airport towers to ARTCCs. You need to be certified for various positions, such as ground controller, associate radar controller and radar hand-off controller. You are required to pass annual physical examinations, semi-annual performance examinations and periodic drug screenings. Air traffic control positions are highly competitive jobs, and the controller workforce is relatively young.

So this is how air traffic control guides aircraft through the skies. Next, check out what those pilots are up to inside the cockpit.

Inside the cockpit: What are those pilots up to?

How many times have you wondered, "What do the pilots exactly do inside the cockpit?" Basically, they fly the aircraft and get you to your destination safely. However, this involves following a strict routine and completing plenty of tasks. People say that the best seat in the whole jet is the window seat, but the best seats in the aircraft are actually the three or four seats in the cockpit. If you sit here, all of your questions about flying a commercial airplane will be answered – how pilots handle those cockpit instruments; how they navigate across the skies; how pilots takeoff and land; and more!

Even though you cannot sit inside the cockpit for a full flight, let's not leave your questions unanswered. Let me take you on a commercial airplane journey from point A to point B. So sit back, relax and enjoy your flight, inside the cockpit!

Prior to 1926, a person could fly passengers or goods without obtaining a pilot's license.

Before the flight

It's not like they portray it in the movies – pilots get a call two hours before the flight and they have to hurry up to fly it. Pilots know about their flight schedule and legs much before the flight. It goes like this - pilots arrive at the airport an hour or two and before the flight. After arriving at the airport, the first thing they do is paperwork. They have to file their flight plan and program this information into the autopilot and navigation systems. They also double-check all aircraft papers such as weight and balance, aircraft logbooks, licenses and limitations along with fuel and passenger load. Then they meet the crew they will be flying with.

However, on smaller airlines, most crews have flown together on the same flights for years and know each other well. Either the captain or the first officer finishes a walkaround check of the airplane. This visual inspection or walkaround is done by one of the pilots as a final airworthiness check.

Normally, one pilot gets onto the tarmac and walks around the jet, looking for any kind of visible faults. Pilots can be penalized even if the overlook a minor thing such as a burned-out light bulb on the wing. After this check, both pilots check all their systems – more than 100 instruments including fuses, circuit breakers and lights.

Though pilots know they have to check all these things, one pilot reads out items from a printed checklist while the other pilot checks them. The airline company issues checklists for various stages of flight, and they vary from aircraft to aircraft.

> *Buttons . . . check. Dials . . . check. Switches . . . check. Little colored lights . . . check.*
>
> **— Comic character Calvin, of 'Cavin and Hobbes.' fame.**

Boarding

While the pilots check all these systems, the gate agents and flight attendants board all the passengers, including you. The AMEs (Aircraft Maintenance Engineers) complete fuelling and final checks. All these checks are to keep your flight safe from any problems. The lead flight attendant then comes back into the cockpit with a thumbs up. The aircraft is ready to go!

Boarding an Easyjet Airbus A319 at Palma de Mallorca International Airport

While filing their flight plan, the pilots contact airport clearance delivery. After that the pilots contact ground control to ask for clearance to push back from the gate.

> *Try to keep the number of your landings equal to the number of your takeoffs.*
>
> **— Pilot's saying**

Pushback

Pushback is a procedure after boarding during which an aircraft is pushed backwards away from an airport gate by external power. Pushbacks are carried out by special vehicles called pushback tractors called tugs. Although many aircraft can also move backwards on the ground using reverse thrust, the resulting jet blast may cause damage to the terminal building or equipment. That is why a pushback using a tractor is the preferred method to move the aircraft away from the gate. Pilots communicate with tractor drivers using radio or walkie-talkies. The pilots then release the parking brakes, and the aircraft moves back!

Pushback tug at Cape Town International Airport

Taxi

After pushback, ground control gives pilots clearance to taxi from the terminal to the runway using taxiways. Ground control decides this runway based on factors like wind, traffic and the flight's destination. Taxiing means the movement of an aircraft on the ground under its own power whereas during pushback the aircraft is moved by a vehicle. The thrust to propel the aircraft forward comes from its engines.

Air France Airbus A318 taxiing at Manchester International Airport

The pilots push the throttle to a suitable speed, taking into consideration the traffic at the airport and air traffic control instructions. Steering is achieved by turning a rudder with their feet. Larger jet aircraft have a tiller - a small steering wheel in the cockpit of an aircraft used to steer the nose wheel. It is used on the ground when the aircraft does not have enough speed for use of the rudder. The aircraft then taxis towards the runway.

Pilots fly free on all domestic routes, regardless of airlines. All airlines have an agreement to lets each other's' pilots occupy empty seats.

Takeoff

When the pilot is close to the runway, ground control transfers him to tower control. Tower control either gives them clearance to takeoff or 'hold short'. Hold short of a runway means stop before specific signs/marking at the holding point because of traffic that is either landing or has just taken off. After turning onto the runway, pilots complete their before-takeoff checklist which includes raising flaps, setting brakes and other important tasks. They then advise flight attendants to take their positions before applying thrust for takeoff. The aircraft then accelerates down the runway for takeoff.

Before the flight, pilots calculate three speeds that come into play during takeoff –

- V1 – This is the go/no go velocity. Before V1, the pilots can abort takeoff in case of critical failures. However, above V1, the pilot continues the takeoff and returns for landing, as any emergency is much safer if dealt with in the air.
- Vr - After one pilot calls V1, he/she will call Vr or "rotate," which marks the speed at which to rotate the tail of the aircraft downwards.
- V2 – This is the speed at which following an engine failure at V1, the aircraft must be capable of climbing and retracting the gear safely. This speed is actually 30% more than the required speed to takeoff to accommodate any unexpected events like wind changes or engine failures.

These speeds are determined not only by the above factors affecting takeoff performance, but also by the length and slope of the runway and any peculiar conditions, such as obstacles off the end of the runway.

Remarkably, there has been a case where two regional jet pilots actually forget to start the second engine of their jet! The pilots got distracted talking to the control tower and assumed they started the second engine.

Embarrassingly, after applying full throttle, he received an automated warning showing the second engine wasn't working, so they headed back to the gate. They thought the engine was malfunctioning until mechanics found it was never started! The regional airline states the pilots went through additional training and updated their takeoff checklist.

Sometimes, when traffic at an airport is light, pilots may complete their before takeoff checks and also receive their clearance before turning onto the runway. Then, as they are turning, they apply full throttle. This is known as a rolling takeoff.

Once the aircraft reaches takeoff speed, the pilots pull the nose up. Then they retract the gear. Along with that, tower control transfers them to departure control. The pilots then climb to their pre-assigned after-takeoff altitude.

Continental Airlines Boeing 757 just after takeoff at Bristol, England.

Cruise

After the aircraft passes 10,000 feet, the pilots tend to be more relaxed, because the workload is comparatively less.

There is also a rule in aviation called the "sterile cockpit rule". In case you're wondering, a sterile cockpit has nothing to do with the cleanliness of the physical environment inside the cockpit. The sterile cockpit rule is a regulation requiring pilots to refrain from non-essential activities like idle chatter during critical phases of flight like takeoff and landing.

After reaching 10,000 feet, the seatbelt sign is switched off and the pilots switch on the autopilot which is programmed with heading, altitude, speed and route information. Pilots navigate through the skies by using sophisticated global positioning equipment along with the autopilot.

Cruise is a portion of a commercial flight that occurs between ascent and descent phases and is usually the majority of a journey. Cruise ends as the aircraft approaches the destination where the descent phase of flight commences in preparation for landing.

Departure control assigns the pilots a certain cruising altitude which they fly to. This is known as the flight level. This may depend upon factors like traffic and weather. On long haul flights, the pilot may climb from one flight level to a higher one as clearance is requested and given from air traffic control.

There's no reason to become alarmed, and we hope you'll enjoy the rest of your flight. By the way, is there anyone on board who knows how to fly a plane?

— Elaine, speaking over the cabin speakers in the 1980 movie 'Airplane!'

Ever wondered what those white fumes behind commercial airplanes at cruising altitude are? The "fumes" are simply water. The exhaust from airplane engines contains mainly carbon dioxide and water. Carbon dioxide has a very low melting point, and so it remains an invisible gas, but the water vapor readily condenses into liquid or ice after hitting the cold air outside the airplane, producing a long trail of fog. In standard atmospheric conditions, airplanes will produce white condensation trails known as contrails above 26,000 feet. However, atmospheric conditions can vary a lot, so sometimes there will be contrails, and sometimes not. Sometimes they fade away quickly, and other times they turn into regular clouds. In any case, they do not consist of chemical fumes, just water, like other clouds.

Cruise is the level portion of aircraft travel where flight is most fuel efficient. Aircraft fly higher to save fuel. Why? Airplanes use less fuel at high altitudes than they use at low altitudes, because the air is thinner at high altitudes and therefore produces less air resistance to slow the airplane down. Using less fuel saves the airline company a lot of money.

During cruise, pilots have their meals, enjoy the scenery and chat among themselves. However, they get to flying once they receive the instruction to descend.

Descent

Air Traffic Control gives pilots a certain altitude to descend to when they are close to the airport. It mostly depends on the airspace near the airport that they are flying to. For example some airports have mountains and hills around them, while some airports are highly congested and require descents which are designed to avoid conflict with traffic near surrounding airports. Pilots also reduce the speed of the aircraft as directed by air traffic control. Descents are an essential component of an approach to landing.

> *Remember, you fly an airplane with your head, not your hands and feet.*
> **— Bevo Howard**

Approach

After the pilots descend to a lower altitude, air traffic control transfers them to approach control. Approach control gives them final instructions to turn and line up with the runway. To do this, pilots have to fly their aircraft in a certain pattern around the airport. Sometimes if there is bad weather or heavy traffic at an airport, air traffic control instructs the pilots to fly in a holding pattern. Modern autopilots, coupled with Flight Management Systems, can enter and fly holding patterns automatically. If there are no delays, the aircraft starts its approach. The final stage of an approach is called the final approach. There are two types of approaches.

> *"The engine is the heart of an aeroplane, but the pilot is its soul."*
> **- Sir Walter Raleigh**

Visual Approach

During a visual approach, pilots fly the aircraft themselves during final approach and landing. A visual approach is done when the visibility near the airport is good, and there is no bad weather close to it. This type of approach is normally done during the day. However, if the airport has a Visual Approach Slope Indicator, then visual approaches may be done at night too.

US Airways Boeing 757 on final approach to St Maarten Juliana International Airport

The Visual Approach Slope Indicator (VASI) is a system of lights on the side of an airport runway threshold that provides visual descent guidance during the approach to a runway. This system consists of two sets of lights. One set marks the start of the runway, while the other is set about twenty feet behind the first. Each set of lights is designed so that the lights appear as either white or red, depending on the angle at which the lights are viewed. When the pilot is approaching the lights at the proper angle, meaning the pilot is on the glide slope, the first set of lights appears white and the second set appears red. When both sets appear white, the pilot is flying too high, and when both appear red he or she is flying too low.

Pilots often use certain rhymes to help them remember basic information like "red over white, you're all right", "white over white, you're out of sight" and "red over red, you're dead". These lights may be visible from up to five miles during the day and up to twenty miles or more at night!

Instrument Approach

An instrument approach is a type of approach that allows pilots to land an aircraft in reduced visibility or bad weather. During an instrument approach, pilots only have to program the computer and do some basic flying while the computer takes care of everything else from reducing speed to descending to lining up with the runway. The Instrument landing system (ILS) is used for this. An ILS is an instrument approach system on the ground that provides guidance to an aircraft approaching and landing on a runway, using a combination of radio signals and high-intensity lighting to enable a safe landing in bad weather. Instrument approach procedure charts are published for approaches to every runway at airports with ILS systems. These charts, also called approach plates, include radio frequencies and navigational aids which provide pilots with the needed information to fly an ILS approach.

If no seats are available, the travelling pilot can occupy an extra seat in the cockpit that is usually empty.

Landing

Pilots lower their landing gear at about 2000 feet. You hear a 'thunk' sound followed by a whirring sound if you are sitting close to the center of the airplane. In the cockpit, pilots see the gear deploying on their computerized displays. Once the main gear and nose gear is deployed, pilots see three green lights. One pilot calls out "three green". They also set the speed brakes and spoilers along with flaps for landing. After telling flight attendants to take their seats, pilots make their final preparations for landing.

During a landing, pilots normally aim for a spot on a runway called the piano about 1000 feet from the threshold, and exactly align their airplane with the centerline on the runway. The runway threshold is marked by a line of green lights. Pilots have to land with a perfect recipe of throttle, descent and concentration.

"To most people, the sky is the limit. To those who love aviation, the sky is home."

- Anonymous

If you have ever seen an aircraft land, you may have noticed that the tires smoke on landing. This happens because of friction - once the tires hit the rough ground at a high speed, they immediately start spinning. This sudden spinning burns a little part of the tire that hits the ground first. This may make it seem as if airlines go through a lot of tires, but they don't. Most tires can handle hundreds of landings before being replaced.

In Airbus aircraft, there is an automated recording that calls out how high the aircraft is just before landing. It starts from 400 feet and calls out the word "retard" at about 10 feet. No, it's not an insult - the word "retard" is a reminder to pilots to bring the thrust levers to idle (zero thrust) during the landing maneuver, known as the "flare," just prior to touchdown. A "flare" is when pilots raise the nose of the aircraft just a little bit, with zero throttle, so that the aircraft slowly touches its main gear down, and then the nose gear is lowered when the speed decreases.

Immediately after landing, speed brakes are deployed along with the spoilers. Pilots also apply "reverse thrust", which means that the direction of the aircraft's engine thrust is changed to forward by deploying panels on the engines, rather than behind. This slows the airplane down. Thrust reversers are used to reduce wear on the brakes during landing. At about sixty knots, they cancel reverse thrust

Alitalia Airbus A320 landing at London Heathrow International Airport

and bring the throttle to idle. Then they exit the runway to clear it for the next landing or takeoff. Once they exit the runway, tower control, which handles takeoffs and landings transfers them back to ground control.

Ground control then tells them which gate to taxi to.

Gate Arrival

Pilots taxi to the assigned gate using taxiways after touching down. This is the time where flight attendants thank passengers for flying the airline and tell them the temperature and local time outside. After touching down, the aircraft taxis to the arrival gate via taxiways, where the engines are shut down. At modern airports like Madrid's Bajaras Airport, there are automated displays that show the pilots how far the aircraft is from the parking spot. As soon as the aircraft is at the gate, the cargo doors are opened so that cargo can be unloaded by the baggage handlers. Cabin crew unlocks and opens the cabin door so the passengers can exit the airplane.

Flying for the airlines is not supposed to be an adventure. From takeoff to landing, the autopilots handle the controls. This is routine. In a Boeing as much as an Airbus. And they make better work of it than any pilot can. You're not supposed to be the blue-eyed hero here. Your job is to make decisions, to stay awake, and to know which buttons to push and when. Your job is to manage the systems.

— Bernard Ziegler, former Airbus Senior Vice President for Engineering, interview in William Langewiesche's 'Fly by Wire: The Geese, the Glide, the Miracle on the Hudson,' 2009.

Shutdown

Before the passengers exit the aircraft, the pilots complete a final safety checklist. The pilots leave the aircraft after all the passengers have exited. It is standard practice for the captain to leave the aircraft last. Cabin crew and airline staff then enters the airplane so that they can clean the airplane and perform maintenance on it before the next leg of the journey.

Resolving Aircraft Faults

Aircraft Maintenance Engineers (AMEs) are alerted by the pilots if any aircraft faults were detected during the flight. The AMEs take whatever actions are required to resolve these faults before the aircraft returns to flight.

Imagine, pilots have to go through this entire procedure up to five times a day if they fly many legs of the same flight. However, even though the process of flying an airplane might seem mind-boggling to some, it is a routine for pilots.
For them, it's just like driving a car, just larger and with more controls!

After looking at what pilots do inside the cockpit and how they fly a commercial airplane, let's take a look at the aircraft they fly. These are the airplanes that get us to our destination.

"I live for that exhilarating moment when I'm in an airplane rushing down the runway and pull on the stick and feel lift under its wings. You have left the world beneath you. You are inside the sky."

- Gordon 'Gordo' Cooper, Leap of Faith, 2000

The airplanes that get us there

How many times have you sat in a plane and wondered, "How is this 800,000 pound jumbo jet going to get off the ground?" Whenever you get on a 747, you are boarding a gigantic piece of metal capable of carrying 500 or 600 people. It weighs about 800,000 pounds during takeoff. Yet it rolls down the runway and, as though by magic, lifts itself into the air and can fly up to 7,000 miles without stopping. It is pretty incredible when you think about it!

All Nippon Airways Boeing 747 at Tokyo Haneda International Airport

Flying is not a magic trick, even though it looks pretty much like it. It all depends on the way the aircraft is built. The aircraft has engines to power it, wings to provide lift and so many other parts. In fact, there are over six million parts in a Boeing 747, half of which are fasteners! All these parts play a small but important part in flight of a commercial airplane. If you are curious to know what enables a 747 – or any other airplane to fly, then read on.

There was this one principle which was instrumental in those big metal birds carrying hundreds of people in it taking to the skies. It is the Bernoulli's principle.

Bernoulli's Principle

It all started in the eighteenth century when a Swiss scientist called David Bernoulli performed an experiment about aerodynamics. He discovered a principle which explains that an aircraft can achieve lift because of the shape of its wings. They are slightly curved so that that air flows faster over the top of the wing and slower underneath. Fast moving air equals low air pressure while slow moving air equals high air pressure.

Remember physics class? Air always moves from high pressure to low pressure, so high air pressure underneath the wings will therefore push the aircraft up towards the lower air pressure.

There is a part or surface called an 'airfoil', whose shape and orientation controls stability, direction, lift and thrust. A wing is a type of airfoil. This airfoil shape also helps the aircraft overcome the effect of gravity which pulls the airplane down. This is the main reason why aircraft can fly.

The air flowing through a Boeing 767-400 engine can inflate the Goodyear blimp in seven seconds!

Aerodynamic Forces

There are four basic forces which are considered in aerodynamics: thrust, which moves an airplane forward; drag, which holds it back; lift, which keeps it airborne and weight, which pulls the aircraft down.

Thrust is the force required to move an aircraft through the air, overcoming drag (and providing sufficient speed for a wing to develop enough lift to fly). This is normally provided by an engine (more about this later), or propellers on some smaller airplanes. Every action has an equal and opposite reaction according to Newton. For thrust, there is drag; and for lift there is weight.

"Caution: Cape does not enable user to fly."
- Batman costume warning label, Wal-Mart, 1995

Drag slows an aircraft down. It means that there is resistance to airflow and that slows the movement of an aircraft through the air. Immediately after takeoff, the pilots retract the landing gear. This is because the amount of drag produced by the landing gear of a jet is so great that, at cruising speeds, the gear would be ripped right off of the plane.

Lift is the aerodynamic force that holds an airplane in the air. It happens because of the Bernoulli Effect, as explained above. On airplanes, most of the lift required to keep the plane aloft is created by the curved shape of the wings (although some is created by other parts of the structure).

Weight is the downward vertical force created because of gravity. Every object on earth including air has weight. Weight is the force that counteracts lift. These are the four main aerodynamic forces. Now let's take a look at how an airplane is controlled.

The Boeing 747 aircraft has four main landing gear assemblies, each of which has four wheels. It also has two wheels on the nose gear, bringing the total to 18.

Controlling Flight

What good is an airplane that flies, but you can't control it? It will just keep flying until it runs out of fuel and crashes. According to Wikipedia, "The Wright brothers are the two men who are credited with inventing and building the world's first successful airplane and making the first controlled, powered and sustained heavier-than-air human flight, on December 17, 1903." Notice the word "controlled"? This is why the Wright brothers are so famous – they were the first ones to successfully control their aircraft during flight.

In flight, the control surfaces of an aircraft produce aerodynamic forces that control the aircraft. These are known as the 'three principle axes'. No, it's not the axe which wood cutters use - 'axes' is the plural of 'axis'. Three of them are found on any airplane. Moving parts of the fin, tail and wing surfaces changes the curves of these parts and affects their lift (and their drag) and provide forces to control the aircraft.

The three axes of control are pitch, yaw and roll. Parts on the fin called elevators control pitching, a part on the tail called the rudder controls yawing, and parts on the wing called ailerons control rolling.

Now let's look at these three forces in detail.

How does an airplane takeoff? The pilots raise its nose when it reaches a certain speed. This means that they are pitching the plane upward. Pushing forward on the control column will lower the nose of the airplane while pulling backward on the control column will raise the nose of the airplane. This is because when the pilots push the column forward, parts of the fin called elevators of the airplane are lowered. This raises the tail of the airplane, lowering the nose. Similarly, when the pilots pull the column backward, the elevators are raised. This lowers the tail of the airplane, raising the nose. It's that simple.

Aviation is proof, that given the will, we have the capacity to achieve the impossible."

- Eddie Rickenbacker

When aircraft are taxiing on the ground, pilots use a part on the tail called the rudder to steer their aircraft left and right. This left and right movement of an airplane is called yawing. Even though the aircraft turns, the wings stay straight and do not move. It is similar to pitch, except yaw is left and right instead of up and down. The rudder is controlled by rudder pedals near the feet of the pilots.

Say an airplane is in flight and air traffic control tells them to turn to a certain heading. Both pilots turn the control column either left or right and the airplane banks to either side. This action is known as rolling. There are parts on the wings called ailerons which roll an airplane to a side. The pilots change the bank angle by increasing the lift on one wing and decreasing it on the other by raising or lowering ailerons. This difference in lift caused by the ailerons rolls the aircraft left or right. Ailerons are not used while taxiing because you cannot turn the wings when you are on the ground. However, both ailerons and rudder are used most of the times while turning in-flight.

The owner's guide that comes with a $500 refrigerator makes more sense than the one that comes with a $50 million airliner.

This is how an airplane is controlled.

Jet Engines

Can an aircraft fly without anything to power it? Obviously not! Most of the time, we take for granted how easily a plane weighing over half a million pounds lifts off the ground with such ease. How does it really happen? The answer is simple. It's those engines below the wings.

Even though jet engines are also called gas turbines, they still work on the same principle – power is produced by sucking in air at the front and blasting out hot exhaust gases at the back.

It works like this - The engine sucks air in at the front with a fan which has huge blades. A compressor raises the pressure of the air. The compressor is made up of fans with many blades and attached to a shaft.

The blades compress the air. The compressed air is then sprayed with fuel and an electric spark lights the mixture. The burning gases expand and blast out through the nozzle, at the back of the engine. As the jets of gas shoot backward, the aircraft is thrust forward.

Jet engine of an Airbus A330 at Cape Town International Airport

The famous physicist Isaac Newton discovered that for "every action there is an equal and opposite reaction." An engine helps a plane zip through the skies using this principle. The engine sucks in a large volume of air. It then speeds this air up and splits it into two parts.

One part of air follows a path through the different engine components. As this air enters the engine, it is heated, compressed and slowed down. The air then passes through many spinning blades. This air is mixed with jet fuel and ignited, and this mixture catches fire. The temperature of this mixture can be as high as three thousand degrees! The power of this high-energy air causes the turbine blades to turn. Finally, when the air leaves, it pushes backward out of the engine. This causes the plane to move forward.

The second part of air "bypasses" the different components in the core of the engine. It goes through a duct that surrounds the core to the back of the engine where it produces much of the force that propels the airplane forward. This cooler air helps to quiet the engine as well as adding thrust to the engine. This is how an engine works.

Various parts of an airplane take part in making it fly - and helping it stay there.

"The nicer an airplane looks, the better it flies."

- Pilots' saying

Parts of an airplane

If you take apart a commercial airplane, you will find the parts that make commercial flight possible. Each one of these parts has different jobs to do while an airplane flies. There are many important parts of an airplane. All these parts have different functions. Let's look at each one of them in detail.

Fuselage

The fuselage, or body of the airplane, is kind of like a tube which holds all the pieces of an airplane together. It is an aircraft's main body section that holds crew and passengers or cargo. A commercial airplane has a wider fuselage to carry the maximum number of passengers. The fuselage is normally divided into two parts - the upper for passengers and the lower for cargo.

Cockpit

On a commercial airplane, the pilots sit in a cockpit at the front of the fuselage. Passengers and cargo are carried in the rear of the fuselage and the fuel is usually stored in the wings.

Wings

Wings are one of the most important parts of an airplane. The wings generate most of the lift necessary for flight. All planes have wings. Wings have smooth surfaces which are slightly curved from the front to the back or. Air moving around the wing produces the upward lift for the airplane. The shape of the wings determines how fast and high the plane can fly. There are various control surfaces on an airplane.

There is no flying without wings.

— French proverb

Winglets

You must have seen those things on the wingtips of airliners that stick straight up. These parts are called winglets. Winglets produce an especially good performance boost for jets by reducing drag.

Winglet on the wing of a South African Airways 737-800 aircraft

At the wingtip, air from underneath the wing flows up toward the top of the wing in a vortex. This causes drag. Winglets help smooth this flow and reduce the drag. By reducing drag the airplane has better fuel mileage.

Ailerons

Ailerons are parts of the wing which are used to roll the aircraft. They are connected to the backside of the wings. The ailerons are parts on the wings and move downward to push the air down and make the wing tilt up or vice-versa. This moves the plane to the side and helps it turn during flight.

Flaps

During takeoff and landing the airplane's velocity is relatively low. To generate more lift and to avoid objects on the ground, airplane designers try to increase the wing area and change the airfoil shape by putting some moving parts on the wings. The flaps are one of those parts.

Like ailerons, flaps are connected to the backside of the wings. The backside of the wing is called the 'trailing edge'. The flaps slide back and down to increase the surface of the wing area. They also tilt down to increase the curve of the wing.

In addition, the increased area of the flap increases the drag of the aircraft, helping the airplane slow down for landing.

Slats

Just like the flaps are connected to the back of the wing, slats are parts on the front of the wing, called the 'leading edge'. Like flaps, slats move along metal tracks built into the wings. Moving the slats forward increases the wing area which in turn generates more lift or drag during takeoff and landing.

Spoilers

As the name suggests, spoilers 'spoil' the airflow over the wing. Spoilers are small, hinged plates on the top portion of wings. Spoilers can be used to slow an aircraft, or to make an aircraft descend, if they are deployed on both wings. When the pilot activates the spoilers normally after landing, plates on both wings flip up. The flow over the wing is disturbed by the spoiler, so the drag is increased. If drag increases, lift reduces, so spoilers can be used to "dump" lift and make the airplane descend. When the airplane lands on the runway, the pilot usually brings up the spoilers to kill any lift, keep the plane on the ground, and make the brakes work more efficiently.

The airplane is just a bunch of sticks and wires and cloth, a tool for learning about the sky and about what kind of person I am, when I fly. An airplane stands for freedom, for joy, for the power to understand, and to demonstrate that understanding. Those things aren't destructible.

— Richard Bach, 'Nothing by Chance,' 1963.

There are only two reasons to sit in the back row of an airplane: Either you have diarrhea, or you're anxious to meet people who do."
— French proverb

Stabilizers

There are various parts that help to control and maneuver an airplane. Stabilizers are small wings located at the tail of the plane to control and maneuver it. The tail usually has a horizontal piece, called the horizontal stabilizer, and a vertical piece, called the vertical stabilizer. The stabilizers' job is to provide stability for the aircraft, to keep it flying straight. The vertical stabilizer keeps the nose of the plane from swinging from side to side while the horizontal stabilizer prevents an up-and-down motion of the nose.

Flying is not Nintendo. You don't push a button and start over.

Rudder

The rudder is a part of the vertical stabilizer. It is used to deflect the tail to the left and right. It controls yaw – the left to right motion of an airplane.

Elevator

The hinged part of the horizontal stabilizer is called the elevator. It is a surface on the horizontal part of the tail section that moves up or down to help the aircraft ascend or descend in flight. It does this by deflecting the airflow so the tail goes up and down. This part controls pitch – the up and down movement of an airplane.

Landing Gear

Seen those huge sets wheels on a plane just after takeoff or before landing? These sets of wheels are the landing gear. Landing gear usually includes wheels equipped with shock absorbers for landing. Landing gear is raised after takeoff and lowered at about 2000 feet before landing. The Airbus A380, the largest commercial jet in the world, has 22 wheels in its landing gear configuration!

The main undercarriage of an American Airlines Boeing 777 airplane

When I talked to an Airbus representative over at Toulouse, France about this, they told me, that at 18 ½ feet tall, a single A380 landing gear must support nearly 170 tons – the equivalent of holding up five blue whales!

Control Column

What good are all these airplane parts, without anything to control them? The part that controls most of the other parts is called the control column or yoke. The pilot uses the yokes to control the pitch and roll of the airplane.

Yokes come in a variety of shapes and sizes, the most common being of a "U" or "W" shape. This configuration is used in most Boeing aircraft. Some aircraft use an "M" style, such as Embraer jets and the Concorde. Another type is the "side-stick".

A side-stick is a style where a joystick is located to the side of the pilot, instead of the center. This configuration is used in most Airbus aircraft.

Aircraft have different systems that are used in flight – the most common being the autopilot.

Autopilot

In a commercial aircraft, the autopilot is a system that helps to guide planes with little or no input from a human.

In the early days of aviation, aircraft required the continuous attention of a pilot in order to fly safely. As aircraft range increased allowing flights of many hours, the constant attention led to serious fatigue. An autopilot is designed to perform some of the tasks of the pilot.

> *A commercial aircraft is a vehicle capable of supporting itself aerodynamically and economically at the same time.*
>
> **— William B. Stout, designer of the Ford Tri-Motor**

On long flights, the autopilot is almost a necessity, because it is not feasible for a pilot to be paying constant attention to the sky for the entire length of the flight.

So how does the autopilot fly the aircraft itself?

The autopilot is basically a computer. It controls the three control surfaces that determine an airplane's course: the movable panels, called ailerons, on the back of each wing that allow the plane to bank right or left; the tail rudder, which turns the aircraft's nose left or right; and the elevators, which point the plane up or down. On commercial aircraft, the autopilot and auto throttle are controlled by an advanced onboard navigational

Various systems and displays inside the cockpit

computer called the flight management system (FMS). A good analogy for the autopilot is the cruise control mechanism in a car, except that the autopilot does much more than controlling speed.

Autopilots have several advantages. Mainly, they help keep the crew from getting tired, leaving them free to alter the flight plan, keep an eye out for traffic, and monitor the plane's other systems (like hydraulics and air pressure). Autopilots also improve fuel efficiency and passenger comfort, since the adjustments made by an autopilot are more subtle and accurate than those made by hand by pilots.

That's why autopilots are typically engaged on commercial aircraft throughout nearly the entire flight. When human pilots take control - mostly during takeoff and landing, and sometimes in mid flight - it's largely because they need to stay in practice - not because the autopilot would be unable to fly safely.

"Any pilot can describe the mechanics of flying. What it can do for the spirit of man is beyond description."
— Barry M. Goldwater, US senator

Typically, a pilot programs the FMS before takeoff, entering landmarks, altitude, and desired speed; during flight, the FMS uses instrument readings and radio signals from fixed points on the ground to figure out what adjustments are needed to meet the flight plan. If a human is in command, he or she must make the changes by hand; with the autopilot engaged, these adjustments are made automatically.

Autopilots can fly the airplane themselves for the full flight – including takeoff and landing, though pilots prefer to do these themselves.

Autopilot is a system that is a part of the flight management system. The second system is autothrottle.

Did you know that in order for a passenger airliner to takeoff, the total pounds of thrust created by all the engines does not have to be greater than the weight of the aircraft? This is because the wings generate lift, which keeps the aircraft airborne. The engines just need to provide enough airspeed for the wings to create the lift. A 747-400 can weigh as much as 870,000 lbs at takeoff, but all 4 engines collectively only put out 224,000 lbs of thrust.

Autothrottle

Autothrottle is also a part of the FMS. It controls the speed of the airplane by adjusting engine throttles automatically.

This system can conserve fuel and extend engine life by calculating the precise amount of fuel required to attain a specific target indicated air speed, or the assigned power for different phases of flight.

Autothrottle is usually activated and deactivated with a switch. In most cases, there are also specific circumstances in which the autothrottle will shut itself off. The pilot can set the airspeed or thrust that he wants the autothrottle to maintain.

Autothrottle is used to maintain a specific airspeed or thrust automatically, without the pilot having to constantly adjust the throttles by hand. This allows the pilot to climb or descend in the airplane without having to touch the throttles—the autothrottle adjusts the engines as required to maintain the desired thrust or airspeed.

On Airbus planes, the thrust levers themselves don't move with the autothrottles engaged. It can be used in all phases of flight, including landing. Just like the autopilot, autothrottle eases the workload of the pilots.

Aircraft Maintenance

Commercial aircraft make money only while flying passengers or cargo, not while sitting on the ground. Therefore, airlines aim for the highest possible utilization of their fleet. They also try to fly as many flights as they can with an airplane.

Once a flight lands and the passengers disembark, the aircraft is swiftly prepared for the next flight. Mechanics swing into action by reviewing the aircraft log for any mechanical problems noted by the last flight crew. Any problems that compromise the safety of flight are solved first.

> *After several Comet aircraft mysteriously broke apart at altitude, they were grounded until a cause was found. By testing a fuselage in a giant tank of water and subjecting it to many simulated pressurizations, they discovered the cutout for the passenger windows didn't have a large enough radius in the corners, and cracks developed leading to an airframe failure in flight.*

The aircraft's main parts like wheels, tires, brakes, control surfaces are checked. Cleaning crews tidy up the passenger cabin and restock sick bags and magazines. The galleys are resupplied with food and beverages. Fuel is pumped into the wing tanks. Before the aircraft is again ready for departure, one of the pilots performs an exterior walkaround inspection, checking for any conditions that might compromise the safety of flight.

These types of checks are not scheduled. This type of immediate maintenance is performed on aircraft after each flight. But is this enough to keep a large passenger plane safe to fly? Just as your cars need servicing, airplanes regularly require a series of extensive and expensive maintenance checks. These are detailed inspections of the aircraft. The types of checks are - A check, B check, C check, or D check. A and B checks are lighter checks, while C and D are considered heavier checks. Let's look at what these checks exactly are.

A Check

This is the first level of scheduled maintenance. It is normally done at airport gates separate maintenance stations, often overnight. Mechanics open panels and check the oxygen flow, lights and also check everything that is checked during a daily check. This type of check is performed approximately every 500 - 800 flight hours.

B Check

Going higher up the maintenance check levels, this type of check is performed approximately every 3 months. This check is also usually done overnight at an airport hangar. A B check includes all the items covered during an A check along with a slightly more detailed check of components and systems. Special equipment and tests may be required. However, this does not involve detailed disassembly or removal of components of an aircraft.

C Check

The C check is the first of the "heavy" checks. The aircraft is flown to an airline's maintenance base where special engineers, materials, tools, and large spaces are available. This type of check is performed approximately every 12–18 months.

The C check is an extensive check of individual components to check if they are functioning properly. During this check, a visual inspection of airplane areas, components and systems as well as operational or functional checks are done. It is a high-level check that involves extensive tooling, test equipment, and mechanics with special skills. C checks put the airplane out of service for about 3 to 5 days. As always, the C check includes all the lower checks like A and B.

D Check

This is the most comprehensive check for an airplane. This check occurs after long intervals like 4–5 years. During this check, mechanics almost take the entire airplane apart for inspection. This requires even more space and time than all the other checks, and is performed only at a maintenance base.

> The "DC" in DC-3 meant Douglas Commercial, as opposed to a military aircraft which, during the 30's and 40's, Douglas was heavily involved in making. After the McDonnell Douglas merger, they used "MD" such as MD-11, or MD-80.

Once the aircraft is parked inside the hangar at the maintenance base - the maintenance team gets to work. Worktables, platforms, and scaffolds are rolled into position for access to otherwise unreachable areas of the plane. Seats, floors, walls, ceiling panels, galleys, lavatories, and other equipment are opened or removed from the aircraft to permit close inspection. New cabin walls and ceiling panels are installed. Carpets, curtains, and seat cushion covers are replaced. Galley equipment is disassembled, cleaned, and sanitized.

Over time, the jolts of thousands of takeoffs and landings cause cracks in the metal structure of the aircraft. To address this problem, workers examine the aircraft for signs of metal cracks and corrosion. Whole sections of the aircraft's landing gear, hydraulic system, and engines may be replaced.

When the aircraft subsequently leaves the hangar after six weeks it is better than new: not only will most of the parts have been repaired or exchanged, all product improvements in the technology and comfort that have been launched by the manufacturers of the aircraft will have been installed.

Interestingly, a D check involves the samples of the aircraft's fuel and its hydraulic fluids being sent for laboratory analysis. If micro-organisms are found in the fuel sample, antibiotics are prescribed! To kill fungi and bacteria that can get into fuel tanks through the air, water, and fuel—the tanks are treated with a biocide, a form of antibiotic. This treatment is important because these microbes can corrode the protective coatings on the surface of the tanks. Fuel probes in the tanks can also be affected and thus cause a big problem - the pilots may receive inaccurate fuel gauge readings.

A D check may take over a month to complete!

It is reassuring to see how much expertise and technology go into keeping the aircraft, and you, safe in the air.

Painting the Aircraft

A small part of the experience of flying on commercial airplanes depends on the colors the aircraft is painted in. How would you feel flying in an unpainted jet? How commercial aircraft are painted is a matter of choice for the airlines which are operating them. Each airline has its individual design, called livery, which distinguishes them from each other. There are lots of airlines, and an equal number of paint schemes.

> *"That's not flying, that's just falling with style!"*
> *- Woody, regarding Buzz Lightyear, in the 1996 movie Toy Story*

Though painting large aircraft is a long and complex process, it is fairly similar to the way a car is painted. Let's take a look at this process.

Firstly, all important sensors, windows, landing gear and door seals are covered so that they don't get damaged or painted. Next, any kind of contamination is removed by a special chemical compound. This is also done by sanding the aluminum. After that, the aluminum is etched so the paint will hold better on it. This etching chemical is later washed off with water.

The plane is then sprayed with an anti corrosion paint using a paint gun, and some parts like screws, bolts or rivets are individually coated. Paint specialists focus on one area at a time while painting aircraft. They cover the rest of the aircraft with normal brown paper. The first layer of paint is applied to the aluminum.

Layers of paint are applied depending on the paint and the manufacturer policy. This painted airplane is left to dry. After that, the paint is lightly sanded to clean any imperfections.

The next step is the most important part of the process– painting the livery. The livery is applied to the aircraft according to the airline specifications. The paint is then glazed to make it extra shiny.

While painting a commercial airplane, the paint thickness is kept to a bare minimum because of the weight. Commercial aircraft may have up to six layers of paint!

This is how commercial aircraft are painted.

Airplane liveries

Most airlines place their own logos and markings on their fleet of jets.

An airline is a business, and it has an image to present to the public. That image is used on the planes as it is used on uniforms, stationary, business cards, even utensils used on board.

Some airlines paint their aircraft in colors other than their standard company livery. This is called as a "special livery".

Many airlines have painted their aircraft in special livery.

The characteristic Olympic Rings logo of Olympic Air

Southwest is known for its "Simpsons" and "Shamu the Whale" livery, while Air France is known for its "Pepsi" livery painted on the Concorde. Of course, these are only a few examples of special liveries – there are many more.

Airplane Makers

Airplanes are graceful, elegant and sleek flying machines that get you to your destination. Do you know who makes them?

These are the airplane manufacturers - major companies who have huge facilities where they build aircraft for airlines. These companies have the difficult task of building airplanes that can fly passengers and cargo safely and economically. This is the main reason why there only two major companies that manufacture passenger jets – Boeing and Airbus.

These two plane makers are based in two different continents. Boeing is an American company, while Airbus is a European company

Boeing is an American company headquartered in Chicago, Illinois and is the largest global aircraft manufacturer by revenue, orders and deliveries. Airbus is a European company and a subsidiary of EADS – it manufactures half of the world's jetliners. Airbus is headquartered in Toulouse, France.

Generally, Boeing aircraft have numbers that start from 7 while Airbus aircraft have numbers that start from 3.

Airbus and Boeing are two companies with fundamentally different products, based on almost opposite visions of the future. Airbus believes that technology should have ultimate control. In emergencies, Airbus planes do not allow pilots to override airplane limits. Boeing's position is that the pilot should have the final say. Therefore, it allows pilots to override any control in case of an emergency.

Boeing and Airbus have a sort of rivalry between each other. After these two come the smaller companies that manufacture regional jets, like Embraer (based in Brazil), Bombardier (based in Canada), and Saab (based in Sweden).

The final assembly point of Airbus aircraft is Toulouse, but the aircraft is a product of many European nations building parts of the aircraft, and then shipping the sections to France for final assembly.

Fly By Wire

There is a major debate going on in the aviation industry in recent times - should pilots or a computer have the ultimate control over the airplane during an emergency?

Airline passengers can't see it, but this is the most significant difference between Boeing and Airbus planes.

Airbus uses "fly by wire" technology in most of its airplanes. Fly by wire simply means that computers on the plane transmit the pilot inputs into electrical signals that are sent through wires. These signals move the control surfaces. Some Airbus pilots describe this technology as, "If you want the airplane to turn, it will turn by itself".

On conventional planes though, the flight-control surfaces are moved by hydraulic devices controlled by cables that run through the airplane.

The fly by wire system is extremely reliable, accurate and almost free from human errors. It's like having power windows on your car – it reduces the pilot's workload. There are so-called "cues" that tell the pilot the plane is approaching certain speed, load or attitude limits. For example, as the jet nears its stall speed, much more force is needed to pull back on the control column.

Airbus also eliminated the control column, or yoke, that is used on all Boeing jets. Instead, Airbus pilots control the plane by moving a small, hand-held joystick off to the side.

If any instrument or part of the aircraft malfunctions or fails, the computers issue warning signals to the crew to take corrective action.

And above all, if a pilot makes a mistake during a flight, the computers issue a warning to the pilot to rectify the mistake, and the computer even locks the relevant control if the safety limit is passed.

The fly by wire cockpit of the Airbus A320 aircraft

Boeing, on the other hand, believes pilots should have the ultimate say. On Boeing jets, the pilot can override onboard computers and their built-in safety limits.

Fly-by-wire was used on jet fighters and on the supersonic Concorde earlier. The first Airbus plane with the technology was the A320, which entered service in 1988.

Newer Boeing planes like the 777 and the 787 also use fly-by-wire technology.

So now you know about the airplanes that get you to your destination. Get to know more about the fear of flying and airplane disasters in the next chapter.

You can be in London at 10 o'clock and in New York at 10 o'clock. I have never found another way of being in two places at once.

— Sir David Frost, Concorde regular flier

The scary part of flying

Reconstruction of Trans World Airlines Flight 800 wreckage in a hangar

Do you ever get the hibbie jibbies when flying? You'll be glad to know that you are not alone. In fact, aerophobia is one of the most common fears that grips the air bound voyager. Although the degree of fear ranges from mild anxiety to complete hysteria, the reasons typically don't vary as much. There are only four main reasons for fear of flying, which I like to call "the four T's". They are turbulence, terrorism, takeoff and touchdown.

Most of the people who are afraid of flying are paranoid about at least one of these things. In this chapter, we'll look at why some folks are afraid of flying and how they can deal with it. We'll also see why aviation accidents happen. But first, let's look the most common argument – is flying in an airplane safer than driving in a car?

Airplanes vs. Cars

The showdown between airplanes and cars has been going on since a long time. The topic of this long standing dispute is a very simple one – "is flying in an airplane safer than driving in a car?"

Dr. Barnett of MIT compared the chance of dying from an airline accident versus a driving accident, after accounting for the number of people who drive each day. Can you guess what he found? You are nineteen times safer in a plane than in a car! Every single time you step on a plane, no matter how many times you fly, you are nineteen times less likely get killed than in your car.

On an average, the annual risk of being killed in a plane crash is about 1 in 11 million. Compare that to the annual risk of being killed in a motor vehicle crash, which is about 1 in 5,000. Based on these numbers, flying seems safer than driving.

> *Aerodynamically, the bumble bee shouldn't be able to fly, but the bumble bee doesn't know it so it goes on flying anyway.*
> *- Mary Kay Ash*

After discussing the long-standing dispute of the risks of airplanes versus cars, let's take look at the four main reasons for fear of flying – the four T's, in detail.

Turbulence

Have you ever experienced turbulence? Sometimes, it feels as if the turbulence is so heavy that the aircraft is going to drop out of the sky and get torn apart. This can never happen, even though it does seem like it. The aircraft is designed to withstand much more pushing around than it will ever encounter. The pilots will usually not even take the plane off the autopilot because most modern aircraft are perfectly capable of handling themselves during turbulence. To get rid of fear of turbulence, it is necessary to understand what it exactly is.

People are often frightened by turbulence, because they don't understand what is happening. They get alarmed even after the slightest up or down bump. These bumps are actually caused by slight ripples in the air. It's just like potholes or bumps on a road. Small disturbances in the air can make a plane ride feel uncomfortable, but there's no real danger.

> *Flying is awful, there's nothing to do when you're up in the air. I bloat up, my skin gets dry, and when we hit turbulence, I'm terrified.*
> **- Daniela Pestova**

Modern airplanes have to be designed and built to comply with rigorous safety standards which are set out by independent aviation authorities. Airplanes and their equipment are manufactured by systems also monitored by aviation authorities. Once built, they are then tested in flight before being given a final seal of approval. They are built to withstand many more stresses and strains than they will ever encounter in flight - the safety margins are enormous. Aircraft are intended to be in the air - it's what they were made for.

You can follow some simple tips to deal with a bumpy flight.
- Take medicine if you have air-sickness
- Drink lots of water
- Get a window seat
- Distract yourself by listening to music

Terrorism

The second thing people are afraid of when it comes to flying is the threat of terrorism. Of course, terrorists have been around for years, and they have a history of using aircraft for bad purposes, the most notable being 9/11.

South tower of World Trade Center explodes after the United 175 crash

It is also important to look at what happened as a result of 9/11. Increase in fear of flying due to terrorism in turn lead to a huge increase in airport security. Police presence at airports has increased now, and any bags that are left unattended are quickly labeled "suspicious packages." Even though people know that aircraft safety is a priority and security measures are more stringent than ever, they still worry.

Did you know that airplanes now have bullet-proof doors on the cockpit to prevent terrorists getting inside? Pilots have a security camera so they can see if it is safe to open the door to the cockpit. Police presence has also increased at airports worldwide. Not all are in uniform, so even though you cannot see them, they can see you.

> *I don't have a fear of flying; I have a fear of crashing.*
>
> **- Billy Bob Thornton**

There is also some paranoia created because of terrorist attacks on airplanes. A good example of this is when a plane was forced to land because the flight crew saw a discarded sickness bag with the letters BOB on it. The crew thought it meant "Bomb on Board".

Flights often have an Air Marshal on board. These are folks in plain clothes who look like normal passengers - so nobody will know that they are there. Their job is to serve and protect passengers during the flight in case of an emergency.

Airline security is at least ten times safer now than it was twelve years ago; but people still wonder why it took something horrifying like 9/11 to increase safety.

Takeoff and Touchdown

These are the two most important phases of flight. Touchdown means landing. People are afraid of these phases because they experience certain fears - one is the fear of flying itself when you are up in the air and the other is the fear of crashing.

However for some the fear is not being up in the air it is the getting there and the coming back down again. This has something to do with the movement of the stomach and the popping of ears as the plane ascends into the air. Some people do not like the feeling of temporarily losing touch with the ground.

Airplane Sounds

An unexpected in flight "bong" or "thunk" can easily scare a nervous traveler. If you are one of them, then this part is just for you.

Let's take a seat in the cabin of an airplane, and explore the sounds and experiences you hear and sense on a commercial airplane journey.

On the ground

At this point, you are in your seat, while the pilots are busy checking all the systems. The airplane is plugged in to the airport's power so that the air-conditioning, lights and other systems can run. Sometimes, this power is supplied by a small jet engine called the Auxiliary Power Unit (APU).

Just as your airplane departs the gate, the lights start blinking and the air conditioning shuts off. This happens when pilots switch the electrical current from the APU or airport power to the engine generators. Your plane is then "pushed back" from the gate. During push back you may hear "clunking" noises. These sounds are heard when a really strong tractor used for pushback attaches itself to the aircraft.

While you're taxiing to the runway, you may hear noises as the flaps and slats are lowered to assist in takeoff. You may notice the wings bounce a little while taxiing – don't worry. These wings are flexible enough to give you a smooth ride without breaking.

Once the airplane is on the runway, you hear a "ding"; this is to notify the flight attendants to get seated for takeoff. Once everything is ready, the pilots apply power. You will hear a loud "roar" as the jet engines spool up. Sometimes the whole aircraft starts to shake. The takeoff roll down the runway is normally about 20-30 seconds. For some nervous passengers, this is the worst 20-30 seconds of the whole journey.

In the air

After a few moments the nose of the plane tilts up and everything gets quieter and smoother as you lift off the runway. Even this climb might seem steep to someone, but pilots can only raise the nose of the airplane up to fifteen degrees, and the maximum is twenty degrees. If air traffic control instructs the pilots to turn immediately while climbing, this may seem extreme to someone too.

After this, pilots raise the landing gear to streamline the airplane. If you are sitting over the center of the airplane you may hear the thump of the landing gear retracting.

Shortly after takeoff you may feel a sinking sensation, that happens when the flaps are retracted (again with a whirring sound), allowing the plane to accelerate. You may also hear the engines throttle back because the aircraft does not need as much power to climb as takeoff. You may even feel as if the aircraft is dropping, but it is not. The airplane is still increasing in speed and altitude, but our body feels otherwise.

Next you might hear another "ding" or notifying the flight attendants it is safe to leave their seats. They go and take the food out from the storage area and heat it up for you. You might hear another "ding" when passing 10,000 feet. Normally, this is the altitude where the seatbelt sign is turned off.

For the duration of the flight, you may hear lots of dings, especially on a long-haul journey. This happens because the passengers press the flight attendant call button whenever they want something or need assistance.

About 40 minutes from landing, the pilots will start descending. You hear another chime as the airplane passes through 10,000 feet and the seatbelt sign is switched back on.

Some people are unnerved when the engine sounds seem to cut out (usually during a descent towards the airport). The pilots reduce the engine's thrust (normally to idle), in order to descend to the proper altitude to prepare for landing.

During approach for landing the pilots will need to slow down to fit into the traffic flow. To do this they may extend the spoilers partially. These panels block airflow over the wing causing drag. You may feel a slight vibration while slowing down.

More noises to expect would be the whine of the flaps extending and a bump similar to the one after takeoff occurs just prior to landing, when the landing gear is set for landing, normally at 2000 feet. Once the landing gear extends you will hear more sounds of air rushing by because the landing gear creates drag.

Close to the ground

Landing is probably the scariest part of flight, and can be compared with the fear passengers experience during the takeoff roll.

Cross-winds can make the plane pitch slightly from side to side during landing. Pilots are able to take these movements into account and it is generally not a problem, though it can be unnerving to feel the plane cabin pitch from one side to another as the ground approaches or even after the wheels first touch the tarmac.

You sometimes hear some increase in the pitch or volume of the engines. Pilots may increase throttle before landing, which is a part of the small adjustments needed to make as smooth a landing as possible.

Arrival

If a landing is discontinued for reasons such as conflicting traffic, weather, or runway obstacles like stray animals, it is called a missed approach or go-around.

> *A Boeing aircraft takes off or lands every 2 seconds somewhere in the world – all day, every day!*

A missed approach can unnerve even the most seasoned traveler. Missed approaches are rare, but you should know that the crew is doing the right thing for your safety. When pilots need to go around, they will add full power, start climbing, and retract the landing gear and flaps. Depending on the reason for the missed approach, they will return for another approach, hold, or divert to a nearby airport. Pilots are well trained for these events and you shouldn't be concerned.

Most of the time, you land safely without any problem.

It is not uncommon to hear wheels squealing as they first hit the tarmac upon landing. Landing is the most violent part of the flight. The spoilers are fully deployed. Brakes are applied and flaps are extended, creating what can best be described as a small roar. This noise seems heightened because the "ear-popping" that occurs in most fliers ears during landing makes those sounds louder.

Ever had airplane earache? This uncomfortable side effect of flying happens because of unequal pressure on either side of the eardrum due to altitude changes when the airplane takes off or lands. An easy way to counter this earache during takeoff and landing is to pinch your nose, close your mouth and gently try to exhale. This is called the Valsalva maneuver. This equalizes the pressure on both sides of the ear drum, stopping the earache. But remember to do it slowly and continuously.

It is also not uncommon for things to shift during landing. The cabin may shake slightly and baggage in the overhead bins shift, creating noise that can be loud enough to make it seem that something is going to break off the plane. These sounds die down quickly as it only takes most commercial planes a few seconds to decelerate after touching down.

> *There are no accidents and no fatal flaws in the machines; there are only pilots with the wrong stuff.*
> **— Tom Wolfe, The Right Stuff, 1979**

Once the plane has slowed it taxis clear of the runway. The engines come out of reverse, the flaps and speed brakes are retracted, again with a whirring sound, and the plane taxis to the gate. Before the engines are shut down, the electrical current is transferred back to the APU or airport power from the engines, leading to a flicker of lights.

These are all the sounds you may hear on a commercial flight.

Why do airplanes crash?

Airplanes are one of the fastest and efficient ways to travel. There is one problem though – airplane disasters. Airplane crashes are rare, but when they do happen they can be very devastating. You cannot stop disasters from happening, there's no harm in knowing what causes these accidents – and how we can try and prevent them.

Airplane accidents can be minor, like a part malfunction on the ground, or they can be very severe, causing a plane to fall from the sky and hit the ground below.

US Airways Flight 1549 landed in the Hudson river after an engine failure

Although popular opinion may suggest that aviation accidents are caused by "bad luck", there have been many situations where these incidents can be completely avoided through careful preparation and safety techniques – a good example being the successful ditching of a commercial jet in the Hudson River.

Disasters don't just happen. Every airplane disaster is the result of a series of small mistakes - like a chain reaction. For all accidents involving an airplane, there are a number of common causes that can influence a plane to crash. These reasons range from pilots or air traffic control errors to airplane instrument malfunction to bad maintenance. Let's take a look at some common causes of airplane disasters.

One question asked by everyone afraid of flying is "If the black box (flight data recorder) is so strong, why don't they make the whole airplane out of it?"

Basically, commercial airplanes are designed to meet and exceed the normal stresses that they encounter in the air. Newer airliners are built with composite materials that are far stronger and more flexible than traditional aluminum.

The black box or flight data recorder usually survives crashes because of its construction not because of its material. There's nothing magical about the material flight data recorders use. They are made mainly of titanium and or stainless steel and covered in fire resistant paint. If you make an entire airplane out of titanium it will not only be insanely expensive but also heavy. Even if you hit the ground at speeds airliners fly at, you have a very low chance of survival anyways.

When most people make mistakes at their jobs, others do not suffer. This is not the case with pilots. When pilots are negligent or make errors while on the job, there is the potential for hundreds of lives to be lost. Pilots receive extensive training designed to prepare them to handle a wide variety of situations, but there are times when mistakes are made.

> *"Pilots take no special joy in walking. Pilots like flying."*
> - **Neil Armstrong**

Aging aircraft may experience structural defects from general use and lack of maintenance. When these problems go undetected, the lives of passengers and flight crew are endangered. There has been a case where a piece of tape was accidentally left over the static ports (parts that relay important information like airspeed and altitude to the pilots) after cleaning the aircraft. This eventually led to the crash. A maintenance employee left the tape on by accident.

The third and one of the most avoidable reasons is fuel mismanagement. Fuel mismanagement can cause an aircraft's fuel tanks to run dry. Fuel exhaustion takes place when the aircraft is completely out of fuel. Fuel leaks could also happen even when the airplane is properly fueled. When pilots act accordingly, disasters caused because of fuel leaks can be avoided. A good example of this is of Air Transat Flight 236. The Airbus A330 aircraft lost all power and hydraulics because of fuel starvation, but the pilots managed to get the jet safely on the ground – with no fatalities.

Accidents also happen because of bad passengers – like hijackings. Some accidents happen because of faults in the very design of the aircraft. There are many more causes of an airplane disaster.

> *I do not use airplanes. They strike me as unsporting. You can have an automobile accident—and survive. You can be on a sinking ship—and survive. You can be in an earthquake, fire, volcanic eruption, tornado, what you will—and survive. But if your plane crashes, you do not survive. And I say the heck with it.*

> **— Isaac Asimov, quoted in J. Winokur's The Traveling Curmudgeon, 2003.**

Any of the above reasons can lead to tragic accidents, causing harm to many innocent victims. Frustratingly, many of these crashes could have been prevented by closer attention to detail and a commitment to safety. The airline industry should make sure that these mistakes do not happen again.

> *Will someone please explain to me the logic that says we can trust someone with a Boeing 747 in bad weather but not with a Glock 9 millimeter gun?*

> **— Georgia Senator Zell Miller, during debate in the U.S. Senate regards approving guns in cockpits**

The media and airplane disasters

Why do aircraft accidents get a lot of media coverage?

Aviation crashes have had a long history of being glorified by the media. Airplane crashes are big events. After all, they involve a big transportation vehicle, carrying many people, at high speeds, and when they crash, the result is utter destruction, fire, billowing smoke, and thousands of pieces scattered over a large area.

It is also because the media only reports unique and rare events like airplane disasters. The media wants news stories that will catch the reader's eye – airplane disaster stories are pretty good at that.

Though there is speculation about certain topics, the media is accurate in most of their reporting. Have you read articles in the paper dealing with your industry or profession? Are they accurate? The media tries, but generally does a bad job of getting all of the facts straight. They can't be experts about everything, and aviation is a complex subject.

> *The man who flies an airplane ... must believe in the unseen.*
> *— Richard Bach*

In the next chapter, get ready for a trip to check out the past and future of airlines.

The History (and future) of Airlines

You have seen how airlines work – but do you know who started the first airline? What is the future of commercial aviation? All of these questions are about to be answered in the next few pages.

In this chapter, we'll embark on a journey to check out the history and later the future of aviation. First, let's look at the history of commercial airlines.

Wheels up: The world takes flight

Since a long time, humans have looked at birds fly – and wanted to fly themselves. Wings made of feathers or light-weight wood was attached to arms to test their ability to fly. The results were often disastrous as the muscles of the human arms are not like birds and cannot move with the strength of a bird.

There were various successful glider flights in the nineteenth and twentieth centuries, but nobody could achieve powered and controlled flight. Then the Wright brothers came along.

Two brothers called Orville and Wilbur Wright were very deliberate in their quest for flight. First, they spent many years learning about all the developments in flight. They completed detailed research of what other early inventors had done, and found out what their mistakes were. One important thing they learned is how the wind would help with the flight and how it could affect the surfaces once up in the air.

Finally, they completed the world's first heavier-than-air powered flight at Kitty Hawk, North Carolina in 1903.

The distance of the Wright brothers' first flight at Kitty Hawk, NC, was only 120 feet, less than the 150-foot economy section of a modern day Boeing 747-400!

First successful flight of the Wright Flyer, by the Wright brothers at Kitty Hawk, North Carolina. Orville Wright was at the controls of the machine, lying prone on the lower wing

During the next century, many new airplanes and engines were developed to help transport people, luggage, cargo, military personnel and weapons. Commercial aircraft that could carry tons of people were built due to this "first flight". Even the term "wheels up" - signifying the landing gear that is raised after takeoff - was coined after this historic flight!

The first animal aviators were a sheep, a duck and a cockerel that were sent aloft in a hot air balloon in 1783.

The first airlines

The world's first passenger airline, DELAG, a German airline, was established in 1909. It used airships called Zeppelins to transport passengers and cargo. This was the start of the commercial airline industry.

Later, some airlines which did not use airships were founded. Some of them still exist! They are Netherlands' KLM, Colombia's Avianca, Australia's Qantas, Czech Republic's Czech Airlines, and Mexico's Mexicana.

It is said that two wrongs do not make a right, but two wrights do make an airplane.

The 1920's

The 1920's was an important decade for commercial aviation. It was the Post Office and airmail delivery that gave the commercial airlines their true start. In the early 1920s, the Post Office had used mostly railroads to transport mail between cities. By 1925, only seven years after the first official airmail flight, U.S. Post Office airplanes were delivering 14 million letters and packages a year and were maintaining regular flight schedules. This gave commercial airlines their true start.

Various airlines were started all over the world. During the 1920s, travelers could still cross the country faster by train than by air. This was because airplanes had to fly around mountains, unlike today; they could not fly safely at night, and had to land frequently to refuel.

Flying by air was uncomfortable and some passengers wore overalls, helmets, and goggles. The airplanes were just thin sheets of metal, rattling in the wind, and passengers stuck cotton in their ears to stop the noise. Cabins were unpressurized—passengers chewed gum to equalize the air pressure. Nevertheless, more and more people were flying. Businessmen comprised most of the passengers, and more and more companies would pay for their employees to travel by air.

The 1930's

Airlines became even more popular in the 1930's than they were in the 1920's, with more and more people taking to the skies. Profitable passenger airlines were realized in the 1930s.

Ford and Boeing were the main manufacturers of aircraft in the 1930's. Ford had a Trimotor airplane, nicknamed the "Tin Goose" because of its metal skin, and was one of the planes used for commercial passenger air travel. Boeing introduced an airplane called the Model 80 in 1928, which also was designed for passenger transport.

> *Angels can fly because they take themselves lightly.*
> — *G. K. Chesteron, 'Orthodoxy,' 1908*

In the early days of passenger flight, airlines realized that they needed to keep passengers happy and encourage them to return once they were brave enough to fly. At the start of the 1930's, some airlines employed male crew members, known as cabin boys or stewards on their flights. These men loaded luggage, reassured nervous passengers, and helped people get around the plane.

Boeing Air Transport changed everything when they introduced female flight attendants, who had to be certified nurses. These women, called air stewardesses, attempted to make passengers more comfortable during a flight. They offered them water, a sandwich, and sometimes chewing gum to help relieve ear discomfort. They also carried baggage, took passenger tickets, checked for gasoline leaks, and tidied up the cabin after a flight.

Did you know that airlines started the credit card industry? 1936, the airline industry created the Air Transport Association, which brought passengers the Air Travel Card. After a $425 deposit, the card allowed travelers to "buy now, pay later" at a 15 percent discount. This type of card was first offered by American Airlines. This was the start of the credit card industry.

Flying across oceans

One of the most traveled and important air routes in world is the one connecting the United States and Europe. Since the advent of commercial air travel after World War I, airline entrepreneurs had been exploring the possibility of flying transatlantic routes.

The airplane has unveiled for us the true face of the earth.
— Antoine de Saint-Exupéry, 'Wind, Sand, and Stars,' 1939

To conquer the Atlantic Ocean was to link Europe and the Americas, the two great industrial centers of the world of the time. This feat was difficult because the Atlantic presented major challenges for aviators due to unpredictable weather and the lack of stopping points for fuel and amenities along the way.

Pan Am, TWA and Lufthansa were some major airlines that flew across the Atlantic Ocean connecting the United States and Europe.

After the war

Airline businesses were beginning to explore new ideas for their passengers, but a major setback – World War II - affected this evolution. However, the progress of the airline industry was significantly accelerated after the war. Did you know that BMW initially produced airplane engines?

Transatlantic air travel in the immediate postwar years remained a novelty, but it offered significant advantages over sea travel. A usual journey by sea across the Atlantic took about five days, while air travel cut that down to less than half a day. Events in the postwar era also led to a rise in commercial cooperation between Western European countries and the United States, which increased tourism and made air travel easier.

While American air services dominated transatlantic routes at the end of World War II, eventually European carriers began to take advantage of the growing market. By the end of the 1940s, Scandinavian Airlines (SAS), KLM, Air France, and Swissair all were carrying passengers across the Atlantic as part of a new postwar air travel boom. This was a stark contrast compared to the last ten years - the transatlantic route was a rarely traveled passenger route, but by 1950, it had become the world's number one route in terms of traffic and produced high revenue and competition among airlines.

The Atlantic had finally been conquered for the common passenger.

Cambrian Airways Vickers Viscount 701 at Bristol Airport

It's only when you're flying above it that you realize how incredible the Earth really is.

- Philippe Perrin

The jet engine era

The jet engine was a technology that revolutionized air travel around the world. Unlike the old propeller-driven planes, jet planes could fly at tremendous speeds, thus cutting down travel time. Jet-equipped airplanes also could climb faster and fly higher. Airlines were interested in this technology to transport passengers and cargo from place to place.

Airlines in the postwar era knew that jet engines were better than the old propellers in many ways. In spite of that, they did not immediately buy them, because they also had high operating temperatures that required very expensive metal alloy components that ultimately would affect an aircraft's longevity and reliability.

> *The aeroplane will never fly.*
> **— Lord Haldane,**
> **Minister of War, Britain, 1907**

Moreover, jet engines used far too much fuel. The takeoff speed was also low in earlier aircraft which would require longer runways. All of this added up to increased costs. As a result, many airlines did not support the building of jet airliners immediately in the postwar era.

The introduction of reliable jet planes, such as the Boeing 707 and 727 along with the Douglas DC-8 ushered in a new era in commercial aviation. These new planes offered more speed and comfort to passengers and were less expensive than propeller aircraft to operate, especially for long-distance routes.

BOAC 707 at London Airport in 1964

The introduction of jets into commercial aviation profoundly changed the structure of commercial airline management and ground operations and affected how airlines managed their shorter routes.

Jet travel also physically affected passengers: the most obvious effect was the body's inability to cope with swiftly-changing time zones, an experience that introduced a new term into the English language: "jet lag."

The greatest advance in aviation since the Wright Brothers.

— the 'New York Times,' 1961. An overused phrase, used here to describe the start of the Eastern Air-Shuttle between New York and Washington.

Jet engines revolutionized air travel throughout the world. For the airlines, jet travel forced them to establish much higher standards of maintenance that required better facilities on the ground and highly trained employees. For passengers, flights meant more comfort, less noise, and most important, less travel time. Once again, a new revolution in technology made the world an even smaller place. The jet age is still going on till today – until humans explore commercial space travel.

Deregulation

The airline industry today is very different from what it was before 1978. This is because of "airline deregulation".

Until 1978, the Civil Aeronautics Board (CAB) of the United States government, regulated (controlled) many areas of commercial aviation such as fares, routes, and schedules. The Airline Deregulation Act of 1978, however, removed many of these controls. The United States was one of the first countries to officially deregulate airlines. The European Union as well as many other governments have followed suit. After deregulation, unfettered free competition ushered in a new era in passenger air travel.

One plus point of deregulation was that it allowed new start-up airlines to enter the market without having to agree to the demands of the larger established airlines. One of these was Southwest Airlines, started in 1971. It was founded by a shrewd entrepreneur who introduced unconventional methods of management such as low salaries, fewer managers, employees who could perform multiple jobs and stock ownership by all employees. Passengers flying this airline had to pay for meals on planes and were charged for checked-in baggage. Fares were so low that they were comparable to intercity bus lines. Southwest was like the world's first budget airline.

A great concern with airline deregulation though is the mistreatment of passengers - particularly in the wake of the tremendously popular budget airlines. This is the reason why passenger bill-of-rights have become a hot topic with regard to the airline industry today.

> *No flying machine will ever fly from New York to Paris ... [because] no known motor can run at the requisite speed for four days without stopping.*
>
> **— Orville Wright, 1908**

Airlines today

Air travel today remains a large and growing industry. It facilitates economic growth, world trade, investment. A main part of air travel today is the ever increasing fees.

Today's airlines add new fees almost every day! Their customer service is dropping – you have to pay for meals on almost every airline. Many people joke that they have to go through a knee-replacement surgery after your knees are crushed when the person in front of you pushes his seat back! What's going on?

There is one simple reason why – rising prices everywhere. Fuel, airport gates, fleet and maintenance prices are increasing.

After looking at the history of airlines and airlines today, we'll take a look at what the future holds - for airlines and airplanes.

The future of airline travel

The outlook for the air travel industry is one of strong growth. Forecasts suggest that the number of passengers will increase rapidly in the next few years. For airlines, the future will hold many challenges. Successful airlines will be those that continue to tackle their costs and improve their products, thereby securing a strong presence in the key world aviation markets.

Airlines and airports face escalating costs, revenue growth constraints and an increasingly dissatisfied customer base. By offering passengers a highly differentiated experience and simultaneously enhancing its operational efficiency, the aviation industry can position itself to become and remain profitable in today's business climate.

> *Flight by machines heavier than air is unpractical and insignificant, if not utterly impossible.*
>
> *— Simon Newcomb, 1902.*

Mergers

One thing that is already happening, and will continue to happen in the future is airline mergers. Mergers are the 'joining' of two airlines into one. This typically happens when one airline is either in bankruptcy or on the verge of bankruptcy, and they get bought by another airline. Sometimes it happens to strengthen the airlines and allow them to compete with other airlines better.

If one airline has lots of destinations in a certain continent, then it may merge with another airline which has destinations in another continent. Mergers are better than codeshares because all the routes are consolidated. This is also better for administration.

United Airlines aircraft in new livery after the merger with Continental Airlines

Airline Mergers have their cons as well. Mergers have meant reduced competition from other airlines, reduced routes and higher ticket prices. Add this to the rising fuel surcharges, taxes and fees and we might as well be flying into a future of expensive tickets which only few can afford. This scenario may turn out to be similar to the old times where only the rich could afford to fly.

A recent merger was the one between Continental and United to form the world's largest airline. Northwest recently was taken over by Delta in 2008. In the past, TWA was gobbled up by American. The list of mergers goes on.

Mergers are deals that are happening now, and will continue to happen in the days to come.

> *The present generation will not [fly], and no practical engineer would devote himself to the problem now.*
>
> **— Worby Beaumont, engineer, when asked if man will fly in the next century, 12 January 1900**

Baggage Fees

Airlines today charge fees for checking even a single bag, and the cost of transporting your luggage will continue to rise in the future.

Travelers will have to cram as much as they can into the baggage allowance that airlines offer. The future may have no baggage allowance – you pay for every bag. It's happening already.

Automation in Customer Service

I was checking my flight status on the Alaska Airlines the other day. Later, I had a few questions about my frequent flier miles. I went to the contact section, when I saw a popup – "Ask Jenn". Most fliers are tired of searching through an airline Web site to get the information they need.

Alaska Airlines has a solution - a virtual customer service agent called Jenn. Tell her your question and she will answer immediately in a friendly voice and link you to the relevant Web page.

I was so fascinated by this, that I spent the next half hour asking her random questions from what colors she likes, to what her favorite food is. She replied to all of my questions without complaining. Finally, when I closed the site, I realized that I had not checked the thing that I went to the site for – my frequent flier miles questions.

Yes, this may be the future of customer service. The next step would be to include voice commands instead of text entries. This is the future of customer service – automation.

Standing Seats

An Italian company called Aviointeriors has come up with the new 'SkyRider' standing seat - taking the phrase "put your seatbacks upright" to a whole new dimension. The company says that this configuration that airlines could use to create a 'basic' class would maximize passenger count and profits, while lowering ticket prices.

Even though standing seats may be the future of flying, we can be sure that we will be safe from them for the next decade or so.

New airplanes

New airplanes are being developed by companies. These airplanes are big, faster and comparatively fuel efficient. The Boeing 787 is a jet that is being tagged "the future of flight" because it is made of composite materials.

Aircraft noise continues to be a problem for people living near airports. Future aircraft will be quieter and eco-friendly too. As we move into the future of commercial aviation, pilots may find themselves increasingly surrounded by computers and ultimately replaced in the cockpit. The military is increasingly launching aircraft without onboard pilots, but such aircraft have a very slim chance of being used for commercial aviation.

All Nippon Airways Boeing 787 Dreamliner at Okayama Airport, Japan

Commercial Spaceflight

With the airline industry gearing up to send people to space for sightseeing, one thing is obvious. Airlines do not believe in the phrase, "the sky is the limit".

Virgin Galactic, a subsidiary of the Virgin group, is the world's first ever venture into commercial space tourism. It is giving common people the opportunity to be one of the first ever space tourists.

Virgin Galactic is the world's first spaceline. Virgin Galactic will own and operate its privately built spaceships to transport passengers into space.

These are some things that might just be the future of commercial aviation.

I think nuclear-powered aeroplanes are the answer beyond 2050.

— Ian Poll, Professor of Aerospace Engineering at Cranfield University and Head of Technology for the UK Government's Omega project, 2008

Author's Note

During an airplane flight, have you ever thought that you are flying almost at the speed of sound, and still, you can have a meal and watch a movie? It almost seems like an illusion!

You saw how airlines work, the trip your bag goes through to get to you, how air traffic control guides an aircraft to its destination, and much more in this book. I hope you enjoyed reading Amazing Airlines.

Flying in an airplane is a unique feeling that needs to be experienced to be believed. Even if you didn't really enjoy flying before you picked up this book - I hope you will now.

About the Author

Aditya Palnitkar is a 15 year old from Sunnyvale, California, presently residing in India. He is an avid airline enthusiast. He does not miss an opportunity to fly. He can tell the details about an airplane in the sky by simply looking at it.

Over the years, Aditya has visited or flown through 24 countries worldwide including the United States, France, United Kingdom, Canada, Japan, India, Egypt, Germany, Netherlands, Spain, Portugal, Morocco, Bulgaria, Turkey, Greece, Australia, Taiwan, Korea, U.A.E, Qatar, Singapore, Hong Kong, New Zealand and Malaysia. On his travels, he has read about airlines, talked to pilots, flight crew and ground staff. He has also conducted research, studied flight schedules, analyzed frequent flier plans, observed quality of services and gathered detailed information about almost every airline in the world.

Aditya aspires to become a commercial pilot or an aeronautical engineer. He wants to start his own commercial airline someday. He is also an excellent communicator and a great writer.

Aditya can be reached at aditya@amazingairlines.com

Acknowledgements

The journey from an airline enthusiast to an author of an airline book has been an inspirational one for me. Many people have helped me with achieving this objective.

I would like to start with a special acknowledgement for the encouragement and support given my father Samir, my mother Anuradha and my brother Sahil while I tackled the task of writing this book and my family members, who helped me balance the task of book-writing with my school studies.

I want to thank Patty Wagstaff and Rod Machado for their initial guidance when I started on the book. Research is a very important part of writing a good book. I am indebted to Capt. Nelson Rolo, First Officer Alexander Womack, Capt. Franky Salamanca and First Officer Xavi Rivero for the narration of their first hand experiences of airlines from the cockpit. Their narrations helped me make the book better.

I talked to a number of experts during the writing of this book. I want to thank these experts for their time.

Randy Jahren – Boeing
Shubho Biswas – Boeing
Vikram Vyas – Jet Airways
Cesar Levy – ALLSTAR
William Tedrick – GE Aviation
Lynne Merritt – Airbus
Karen Ellis – Atlanta International Airport
Brigitte Hebert - National Airlines Council of Canada
Carl Austin – Aerosphere

I also spoke with various people over at Airbus, Boeing and Bombardier. I want to thank them for their expertise.

I am grateful to Amit Patwardhan, Jai Rawat, Gaurav Juvekar, Prathamesh Anantwar, Sanjay Swamy and Manasi Nene for conducting a thorough review of the manuscript.

Some of the material in this book was inspired by conversations, email, and suggestions from people. I have credited these sources where known, but if I have overlooked anyone, please accept my apologies.

Aditya Palnitkar
Sunnyvale, California

More Information

If you found this book interesting, you will be happy to know that there are thousands of references on commercial aviation. Check out *www.amazingairlines.com* for a detailed list of interesting books, references and reading material.

I referred to a vast number of pages of material during the creation of this book. I found these references to be very interesting. I hope you do too.

HowStuffWorks.com is a wonderful site that I used very often while researching my book. I read articles by Kevin Bonsor, Tim Crosby, Karim Nice, Tom Harris, Craig Freudenrich, Marshall Brain and Brian Adkins.

I really enjoyed the essays at U.S. Centennial of Flight Commission website at *www.centennialofflight.gov.*

Quotes and facts at *www.skygod.com* by Dave English were very helpful and added to the inset boxes around the book.

The Bureau of Labor Statistics website at *www.blg.gov* had detailed information about flight crews and their working patterns.

Airliners.net is a really popular aviation site. I participated in the forums at that site. This greatly helped my research.

If you want to read more, here are some really cool books. Check them out at a library or a nearby bookstore:

David Anderson and Scott Eberhardt. *Understanding flight.* McGraw Hill, 2001.

Graham Edwards and Gunter Endres. *Jane's Airline Recognition Guide.* Collins-Janes, 2006.

Duane Brown. *Flying Without Fear.* New Harbinger Publishers. 1996.

William and Frank Berk. *Guide to Airport Airplanes.* Plymouth Press, 1996.

John Cronin. *Your Flight Questions Answered by a Jetliner Pilot.* Plymouth Press, 1998.

Stephen Dalton. *The Miracle of Flight. Firefly Books, 1999.*

Dave English. *Slipping the Surly Bonds. McGraw-Hill, 1998.*

Julien Evans. *All You Ever Wanted to Know About Flying.* Motorbooks, 1997.

Layne Ridley. *White Knuckles.* Doubleday & Co, 1987.

Debbie Seaman. *The Fearless Flier's Handbook. Ten Speed Press, 1998.*

Ed Sternstein and Todd Gold. *From Takeoff to Landing.* Pocket Books, 1991.

Art Credits

In this section, I have cited my sources for pictures. I want to thank the creators of the pictures I have included in my book. Many pictures were sourced from Wikimedia Commons. I have tried to be as thorough as possible. However, if I have missed crediting any picture, please accept my apologies.

Index

A

A380 92, 118, 119
A check 123
ailerons 116
Airbus 106
Air Canada 16
airfoil 116
Air France 5, 14, 127, 149
airline deregulation 151
airline hub 11, 12, 43
airline mergers 153
Airlines
    Cargo 9
    Charter 8
    low-cost 7
    major 5
    national 5
    regional 6
Air Marshal 135
Airplane Food 26
Air Traffic Control 15, 79, 93
air traffic delays 7
Air Transat 141
airworthiness 95
Alaska Airlines 155
altitude 33, 74
Amadeus 20
American Airlines 5, 12, 15, 28, 92, 147
Antonov Airlines 9
approach 80, 88
APU 136
Area Control Center 80
ARTCC 80, 93
Ask Jenn 155
attendants 33, 36, 37, 38, 39, 40, 41, 68, 96,
        99, 105, 107, 136, 147
automated kiosk 20
autopilot 119
autothrottle 121
Avianca 35, 146
Aviation jokes 7
Aviointeriors 156

B

baggage handling 42
baggage transport 9
Bajaras 76
bankrupt 8
bar-code 45
B check 123
Bernoulli 110
birds 65, 110
boarding 96
boarding pass 17, 19, 20, 21, 36, 47, 70
Boeing 787 156
Boeing Air Transport 40, 147
Bombardier 128
British Airways 10, 27, 92
budget airlines 152
business travelers 24

C

cabin class 7
call signs 92
cargo aircraft 9
cargo airlines 9, 55
Cargolux 9
carousel 49, 77
C check 123
ceiling panels 124
cell phone 72, 83
central airport 11
charter airlines 8
Chelsey Sullenberger 33
Civil Aeronautics Board 151
class 7, 17
clearance delivery 80, 82, 96
codeshare 14, 15, 16, 153
commercial airlines 3, 144, 146
commercial aviation 38, 78, 144, 146, 150,
        151, 156
commuter airline 12
competition 16, 149
composite materials 140, 156
Concorde 119, 127, 130
concourses 46, 53, 57

Continental Connection 6
control column 112, 113, 119, 129
control tower 79, 81, 82, 88, 93
corrosion 124, 126
cruising 74, 81, 101, 111
customs 50, 55, 57
Czech Airlines 146

D

D Check 124
de-icing 59, 74
DELAG 146
delays 23
Delta Airlines 5, 12
delta.com 14
Denver International 54
departure 86
destination-coded vehicles 43
DHL 9, 57
discounted fares 8
dispatchers 32, 68, 69
domestic airlines 27
Douglas DC-8 150
drag 111, 112, 116, 138

E

El Al 70
elevator 112, 118
Ellen Church 40
Embraer 128
employees 2, 5, 146
empty seats 8, 18, 98
En Route 86
e-tickets 17, 19
European Union 151

F

FAA 23, 65, 81, 93
fare 18
FedEx 9, 10
first officer 30, 70, 95
flag carriers 5
flaps 116
flare 106
flight attendant 28, 36, 41, 137
flight cost 13
flight data recorder 140

Flight Dispatch 75
Flight Management Systems 103
Fly By Wire 129
FMS 121
Ford 147
freight 9
fuel mismanagement 141
Fuel Prices 18

G

Galileo 20
galley 124
gas turbines 113
GateGourmet 28
go/no go velocity 99
gourmet 26
ground controllers 60
Gulfstream International 6

H

Hartsfield Atlanta International Airport 11
hijackings 141
holding short 63
Houston 51
hubs and spokes 4, 11, 12, 13
Hudson River 33
Huntsville, AL 14
hydraulic 59, 124, 125, 129

I

IATA 17, 61, 92
ICAO code 61
ILS 105
in-flight 26, 27, 30, 87, 113
international airlines 6, 9, 11
Isaac Newton 114

J

jet engines 113, 136, 150
jet lag 24

K

Kitty Hawk 144
KLM 5, 92, 146, 149

L

La Guardia 54

landing gear 118
landmarks 121
lift 111
light signals 84
livery 125, 126, 127
logbooks 95
long-distance routes 5
low cost airlines 7
LSG Sky Chefs 26, 28
Lufthansa 148

M

maintenance 23, 34, 55, 59, 64, 66, 68,
        69, 108, 122, 123, 124, 140, 141,
        151, 152
major airlines 5, 9, 12, 13, 39, 41, 43
        70, 148
malfunction 140
Mexicana 146

N

national airlines 5

O

official language 35
operating carrier 15
operating efficiency 13
overbook 19

P

painting 125
Pan Am 148
pitch 112, 113, 119, 138
pivot 47
Plane Train 56
point to point 13
preflight 81
private jet 3, 4, 8
profit margins 8
pushback 97

Q

Qantas 15, 146

R

radio-frequency 46
red-eye 24, 25
regional airlines 6, 9, 14, 100
reservation system 20
reserve pilot 34
retard 106
revenue 5, 7, 18, 128, 149, 153
roll 113
rudder 118
Ryanair 20

S

Saab 128
Sabre 20
Safety Features Cards 73
San Francisco, CA 11
Scandinavian Airlines 149
scanners 43, 45
schedules 2, 4, 11, 44, 146, 151
seat assignment 19
seat demand 18
seat supply 18
secondary hubs 11
seniority 34
Shamu 127
side-stick 119
Simpsons 127
SkyRider 156
slats 117
snow-removal 66
Southwest Airlines 13, 23, 152
Spaceflight 157
spoilers 117
stabilizers 118
Standing Seats 156
Star Alliance 16
status screens 15
sterile cockpit 101
Steve Stimpson 40
Swissair 149

T

takeoff 1, 6, 24, 26, 31, 32, 36, 40, 60, 68, 69, 72, 73, 74, 78, 84, 85, 92, 94, 96, 99, 100, 101, 106, 107, 109, 111, 112, 116, 117, 118, 121, 124, 131, 135, 136, 137, 138, 139, 145, 150
taxi 73, 79, 80, 83
TCAS 93
teenager 2, 40
terrorism 134
thrust 106, 137
ticket agencies 20
tickets 4, 8, 15, 17, 64, 147, 154
Tin Goose 147
touchdown 62, 90, 106, 131, 135
TRACON 79
trailing edge 117
transatlantic 24, 148, 149
transportation 13, 53, 55, 56, 143
travel website 19
Trimotor 147
turbulence 133
TWA 148

U

United 5, 13, 16, 26, 39, 50, 58, 64, 72, 80, 87, 93, 134, 148, 151, 154, 159
UPS 9
US Airways 33

V

Virgin Galactic 157
Visual Approach Slope Indicator 104
volunteers 19

W

weather 13, 23, 31, 32, 33, 36, 40, 60, 65, 66, 67, 69, 78, 81, 87, 88, 90, 91, 103, 104, 105, 138, 148
weight 111
white fumes 102
winglets 116
World War I 148
World War II 149
Wright

Orville 144
Wilbur 144

Y

yaw 112
yokes 119

Z

Zeppelins 146

Made in the USA
Lexington, KY
09 January 2013